Venissa

Be Faithful

Dec 18, 2008

SALE NO

FOR SAL

NOT FOR SALE

Integrity in a Culture of Silence

Samuel Koranteng-Pipim, Ph.D.

NOT FOR

NOT FOR SALE

Integrity
in a Culture
of Silence

Samuel Koranteng-Pipim, Ph.D.

BEREAN BOOKS
Ann Arbor, Michigan

A CAMPUS p.r.e.s.s. BOOK
Publication Resources &
Educational Services for Students

Printed by Review and Herald Graphics,
Hagerstown, Maryland 21740, USA
Copyright © 2008 by Samuel Koranteng-Pipim, Ph.D.
Published by Berean Books, Ann Arbor, Michigan, USA
Printed in the United States of America
All Rights Reserved
First Printing, November 2008

Editing by Ken McFarland
Cover Design and Layout by Elizabeth Oh
Design and Layout Consultants by Jeannie Kim and Ed Guthero

For your personal copy of Not for Sale, or for additional copies,
contact your local Christian book store or mail your prepaid order
($17.99, plus $5.00 shipping and handling in the USA) to:
Berean Books, P. O. Box 2799,
Ann Arbor, Michigan 48106, USA.
Website: www.berean-books.org

For quantity discounts to churches, schools, or groups,
contact the author at the above address or at:
Phone: 734-528-2863; Fax: 734-528-2869; E-mail: skpipim@gmail.com.

Koranteng-Pipim, Samuel
Not for Sale: Integrity in a Culture of Silence / Samuel Koranteng-Pipim

1. Christian Life
2. Integrity
3. Injustice—Religious Aspects—Christianity
4. Contemporary Issues
5. Biblical Teaching
I. Title

ISBN-10: 1-890014-09-5
ISBN-13: 978-1-890014-09-4

CONTENTS

DEDICATION

CAMPUS Missionaries
—Past and Present

You believed that it's possible to change the world
—by being changed.

You challenged the *status quo*
—by putting *quo* in the *status*.

You inspired a generation of youth
—by your excellence, sacrifice, and commitment.

You still believe. You still challenge. And you still inspire!
To God Be the Glory!

ACKNOWLEDGMENTS

TO my wife Becky and children, Ellen & Sam—
Only the good Lord knows how much you've sacrificed for His cause!

And to many friends whose encouragement and unique contributions made this book possible.

THEY INCLUDE
Dan Augsburger
Janet Bell
Olga Brady
Janice Candy Browne
Steve & Tamara Conway
Ron du Preez
Philip W. Dunham
Ed Guthero
Dan Hall
Cari Haus
Jeannie Kim
Tracie Kim
Sula Mazimba
Ken McFarland
Philip Mills
Al & Marion Newhart
Olabisi Obadofin
Liz Oh
Eugene Prewitt
Jay Rosario
Sarah Shim
John Simon
Jerry Thomas
Julia Chappelle Thomas
Narko Tutuo
Paul Yeboah

Each of you invested untold hours and energy either in transcribing, editing, critiquing, cover design & layout, or in praying for this project.

Thank You!

PREFACE

As I read the powerful message of this book, I was not in the least disappointed. Having known the author for some time, I knew what to expect. This great defender of TRUTH and righteousness, this careful "scholar/seeker" has for long carefully established with scriptural authority the parameters of faith and faithful living. His anchor is the Word of God which he holds as the voice of God to hungering souls of every tribe.

One feels safe when reading Dr. Pipim because he carefully articulates truth and confirms it with other inspired witnesses. "Naboth" speaks to us with power and conviction! "Ahab" is uncovered and exposed with thousands of other Ahabs even in our time.

I heartily recommend this volume—especially in these awesome times.

Charles D. Brooks

"Our lives begin to end the day we become silent about things that matter."

Martin Luther King, Jr.

INTRODUCTION

We live in a culture of cowardly silence—a controversy-avoiding society where "getting along by going along" is the way of life. In this culture of silence, we tend to be mute on critical issues or conditions, until our personal self-interests are threatened, or until it is too late.

The tragedy of this cowardly silence is captured in the poem "First They Came," by prominent Lutheran pastor and anti-Nazi theologian Martin Niemöller (1892–1984). Initially a supporter of Adolf Hitler, Niemöller eventually became one of the staunchest critics of Nazism. For his opposition to Hitler's Nazi regime, Niemöller was imprisoned in two concentration camps, where he narrowly escaped execution.

In "First They Came," he describes the consequences of the silence and inaction of many people after the Nazis began the purging of their chosen targets, one group after another:

> "In Germany they came first for the Communists,
>   and I didn't speak up because I wasn't a Communist.
> Then they came for the Jews,
>   and I didn't speak up because I wasn't a Jew.
> Then they came for the trade unionists,
>   and I didn't speak up because I wasn't a trade unionist.
> Then they came for the Catholics,
>   and I didn't speak up because I was a Protestant.
> Then they came for me,
>   and by that time no one was left to speak up."[1]

This sobering poem not only warns against the dangers of apathy but also urges courage in times of crisis.

Regrettably, the culture of our times does not, in general, reward unpopular courage— except long after those displaying such courage have passed from the scene.

How easy it is to honor the heroes of yesteryear from our safe harbors today! How comfortable it is to marry cowards than to be widows of principled nonconformists! And how secure it is to be sheltered in the shade of apathy than to be burned by the battle for right.

To defy today's culture of silence demands the courage of convictions. This is why **NOT FOR SALE** has been written.

This book is a call to personal accountability and principled involvement in the issues that matter. It is an appeal to the "silent majority" who sometimes hold their peace at critical times, when their voices could make a clear difference. **NOT FOR SALE** argues that when we do not act, we are choosing complicity. For, in the words of Plato, "silence gives consent."

This volume grew out of a plenary address I gave at a recent Michigan Men of Faith convocation. The theme for that occasion was "The Want of Men"—a phrase that comes from E. G. White's famous statement:

> "The greatest want of the world is the want of men—men who will not be bought or sold, men who in their inmost souls are true and honest, men who do not fear to call sin by its right name, men whose conscience is as true to duty as the needle to the pole, men who will stand for the right though the heavens fall" (Education, p. 57).[2]

My specific assignment at that Michigan Men of Faith meeting was to speak on the first quality listed in the above quote—namely, "men who will not be bought or sold." The title of this book—**NOT FOR SALE**—was the title I chose for my presentation on that occasion. It captures the thought that jumped out when I reflected on a troubling story recorded in the Bible.

This biblical account begins with a seemingly harmless proposal for a business transaction—a potential sale of some valuable real estate. The business deal falls apart, and, unfortunately, one of the negotiating participants is brutally murdered.

As we investigate the biblical passage more carefully, however, we discover that the story is not just about the sale of real estate. Rather, it highlights an important truth about integrity—about standing steadfastly for principles, regardless of the cost.

As in many other biblical passages, one can derive other surprising applications from the disturbing narrative in 1 Kings 21. For example, besides integrity, the passage also speaks compellingly to the culture of cowardly silence that enables evil to triumph. By drawing attention to some key actors in the story, this account from the biblical past points out possible roles we can choose to play in the climate of our own times—whether in the church or in society.

NOT FOR SALE is dedicated to past and present student missionaries at CAMPUS.[3] These students come from major universities in the country—including Harvard, MIT, Princeton, and Stanford. They are not only sacrificing one year of their education to volunteer as students on secular universities in Michigan but are also paying significant tuition and boarding fees to attend.[4]

I have dedicated this work to these student missionaries because at a time when many adults are silent, the idealism, courage, and selfless actions of this group of young people have inspired a generation to rise up and make a difference in their church and their world. Their strong belief that they can change the world by being changed confirms that serious young people want something far better than the entertainment and low expectations too often offered them.

In a real sense, the integrity described in **NOT FOR SALE** is *about* these CAMPUS missionaries, and the challenge against the culture of silence is *to* them—and to all others, both young and old, who have been inspired by their selfless commitment.

NOT FOR SALE is a call to daily self-examination—and action. It highlights the consequences of the cowardly silence all too often displayed by some otherwise good and well-meaning people. Contending that silence, neutrality, or indifference in times of crisis is a criminal act, if not a betrayal of faith, this book makes an urgent plea against choosing to do nothing in the face of wrong-doing.

Above all, **NOT FOR SALE** is written to give support and strength to those suffering needlessly on account of their principled decisions. Unlike cowardly silence, which puts selfish interests before principle, this book encourages *patient silence*. The two words in this expression are calculated to emphasize the dual traits of gentleness and meekness in the face of injustice and hurt. Patient silence is the quality that enables us to hold on, no matter what. It is that which inspires us to be "men whose conscience is as true to duty as the needle to the pole, men who will stand for the right though the heavens fall."

The times in which we live demand courageous people. More than any other time, ours calls for people of integrity—people who will not be bought or sold. It calls for individuals who would dare to stand up and speak for truth, justice, human rights, and freedom of conscience—regardless of the consequences. For these principles, generations before us fought and died. This is why they are **NOT FOR SALE**!

Samuel Koranteng-Pipim, Ph.D.
Ann Arbor, Michigan
November 4, 2008[5]

NOTES

1 Many versions of Martin Niemoeller's "First They Came" poem exist, both in terms of its origin and in the substance and order of the groups he mentioned. The version quoted above is inscribed on a stone in the New England Holocaust Memorial. Other versions of the poem list groups that were purged by the Nazis, such as: Communists, the incurably ill, Jews, Jehovah's Witnesses, people in occupied countries, Socialists, the trade unionists, the schools, the press, and the Church. These groups were considered "undesirables," to be eliminated.

2 Ellen Gould White (1827-1915) was a woman of remarkable spiritual gifts who lived most of her life during the nineteenth century, yet through her writings and public ministry she has made a revolutionary impact on millions of people around the world. She is considered the most widely translated American author. Her works have been published in more than 140 languages. Although her formal schooling ended at age 9, she wrote more than 100,000 pages on a wide variety of topics—spirituality, theology, education, health, family, etc. But she was more than a prolific author. While the world is only now coming to appreciate her deep spiritual and practical insights, millions have always recognized her as a recipient of the true gift of prophecy. Her life-changing masterpiece on successful Christian living, *Steps to Christ*, has been published in about 150 languages, with well over 100 million copies in circulation. Her crowning literary achievement is the five-volume "Conflict of the Ages" series, which traces the conflict between good and evil from its origin to its dramatic, soon-to-unfold conclusion. It is widely acclaimed as the best devotional commentary on the entire Bible. E.G. White was a founding member of the Seventh-day Adventist, one of the fastest growing Protestant denominations. Hereafter Ellen Gould White would be cited simply as "E.G. White." References to her works are from the standard editions, all of which are available either through Review and Herald Publishing (55 W. Oak Ridge Drive, Hagerstown, Maryland 21740; Phone 301-393-3000; www.rhpa.org) or through Pacific Press (1350 North Kings Road Nampa, ID 83687; Phone: 208-465-2500; www.pacificpress.com). In the USA and Canada, to find a local retailer near you call 1-800-765-6955.

3 CAMPUS stands for Center for Adventist Ministry to Public University Students. A division of the Michigan Conference Public Campus Ministries Department, CAMPUS is based in Ann Arbor, Michigan, near the University of Michigan. CAMPUS describes its approach to ministry in the following way: (1) *Vision*: A Bible-based revival movement, in which every student is a missionary; (2) *Methodology*: Biblical simplicity; (3) *Philosophy*: Academic excellence and spiritual excellence; (4) *Goal*: Double our membership every year; (5) *Watchword*: Each one reach one; (6) *Mission*: To prepare secular university campuses for the imminent return of Christ; (7) *Motto*: Taking Higher Education Higher. For more information, see www.campushope.com.

4 CAMPUS runs a Missionary Training Program in Ann Arbor, Michigan, near the University of Michigan campus. It is a two-semester, hands-on program that combines sound classroom instruction with practical field training in ministry and outreach activities. The classes are taught by dedicated staff and guest instructors. The goal of the Missionary Training Program is to develop godly and effective leaders, brilliant and winsome soul winners, and sound spiritual counselors for college/university campuses and other professional environments. Limited to no more than a dozen serious students at a time, the program duration overlaps with the academic year at the University of Michigan.

5 Perceptive readers will recognize this date as the historic day that the United States elected the first African-American to be president.

PART 1
THE ST

A Visit t

the Pas

"Saying nothing... sometimes says the most."

Emily Dickinson
American Poet, 1830–1886

A BUSINESS PROPOSAL

Ahab, son of Omri, was the seventh king of Israel, who reigned for twenty-two years, from about 876 B.C. to 854 B.C. He was one of the greatest kings of the northern kingdom of Israel. His political marriage with Jezebel, the daughter of Ethbaal, king of the Zidonians, resulted in a fair degree of stability in his kingdom. But it also brought about Baal worship, which compromised the religion of Israel. [6]

King Ahab was a very rich man in his day. Owner of two posh palaces (one in Samaria and one in Jezreel), he had power at his fingertips—the wealth of a nation at his command. But he wanted more. Like so many wealthy people of today, Ahab knew from experience that money doesn't bring happiness, for he was a very unhappy man.

One fateful day, Ahab was found gazing out of his spacious palace window. No doubt he had looked out this window many times before, but this time was different. His wandering and covetous eyes fell on a vineyard—a lush and beautiful one owned by a man named Naboth.

Being a real estate investor of sorts, King Ahab came up with an incredibly "bright" idea. He decided to add Naboth's vineyard to his personal portfolio of farm holdings. The biblical account in 1 Kings 21:1, 2 reads:

> **"And it came to pass after these things that Naboth the Jezreelite had a vineyard which was in Jezreel, next to the palace of Ahab king of Samaria. So Ahab spoke to Naboth, saying, 'Give me your vineyard, that I may have it for a vegetable garden, because it is near, next to my house; and for it I will give you a vineyard better than it. Or, if it seems good to you, I will give you its worth in money.'"**

Ahab's proposal seemed fair. He didn't command or order the owner to sign over the title of the land to him. It was a very courteous request. He took the time to share the reasons for his interest in the property, and he negotiated the deal so that Naboth would not lose out.

"Look, Mr. Naboth," he was saying, "I really need your vineyard [1] for a garden of herbs, because [2] it is near my house. And I'm going to give you a very good deal. As king of the land, [3] I will give you a better vineyard, or [4] I will give you its worth in money."

Naboth's reply couldn't have been more definite: *"The Lord forbid that I should give the inheritance of my fathers to you!"* (1 Kings 21:3)

It wasn't that Naboth disliked Ahab. Nor was it because Ahab failed to make a convincing offer. The simple reason was that *the vineyard was not for sale.* It was a matter of Naboth's faith. He would not sell out His God. He would not trade in his heritage. For *He Himself* also was not for sale.

A MAN WHO COULDN'T BE BOUGHT OR SOLD

Naboth would have gladly obliged the request of Ahab, which seemed so reasonable and appealing. He did not hold a spirit of defiance against the king's governance. And if he had complied, he would have been honored and rewarded by the king. But three reasons stood in his way: his identity, his ancestral heritage, and his spiritual integrity. These were the reasons the vineyard was not for sale.

1. The Vineyard Had to Do With His Personal Identity

Four times in the 1 Kings 21 passage, the owner is described as "Naboth the Jezreelite" (see verses 1, 6, 7, 15). Verse 1 explains Naboth's identity as a Jezreelite by the fact that he "had a vineyard which was in Jezreel." This description is more than a geographical reference. *The vineyard was tied to Naboth's identity.* Who Naboth was, where he lived, and the land were all intertwined. Take away the vineyard, and Naboth had no legitimate identity as a Jezreelite.

And as you know, *identity* cannot be easily bought or sold. Identity is one of the greatest assets of business corporations, churches, and individuals. This is why companies fight to protect their unique brand names. Churches (including our own) will even sue other groups to preserve their identity. People spend their lives in search of their identities—groups and nations as well go to great lengths to define their identities. And, yes, individuals will do anything to preserve (or regain) the reputation of their name. This is also why we fight to preserve historical icons, because our history reminds us from whence we've come, which helps to direct us as to where we will go.

The vineyard of "Naboth the Jezreelite" was a mark of his identity. In Israel were many Naboths, but only one was "Naboth the Jezreelite." He was a Jezreelite, because Jezreel was where he lived, where his allotted land was. Without his ownership of the land in Jezreel, Naboth was a foreigner, outsider, or even a slave. His tie to his identity, moreover, harmed no one. His attachment to his land was not a matter of greed or nostalgia but rather a matter of meaning. Ahab's proposals, no matter how extravagant, were not worth giving up a land that helped define who he was.

But the vineyard represented more than Naboth's personal identity.

2. The Vineyard Had to Do With His Ancestral Heritage

The land was not simply the possession of Naboth as an individual. It was also land that had been passed from generation to generation. In verse 3, Naboth describes the land as "the inheritance of my fathers." Perhaps it was apportioned to his ancestors when Joshua had parceled out the Promised Land, giving a portion to each of the twelve tribes—and then to each family from each tribe. [7]

As it had been the land of his ancestors, so would it be the land of his progeny—sons and daughters who would come after him.

In other words, it was inconceivable and undesirable for Naboth to sell the vineyard to Ahab, because the land was given not just to him but to his entire family—not just his immediate relatives but his whole family that had gone centuries before him and his family that would come generations after him.

In ancient Israel, "the inheritance of my fathers" was land to be a cherished inheritance forever. [8] It was *an everlasting* treasure—a legacy not to be traded in. It was thus considered holy—and to be guarded even at the peril of one's life. It reminds me of the hymn "Faith of Our Fathers."

Faith of our fathers, living still,
In spite of dungeon, fire and sword;
O how our hearts beat high with joy
Whenever we hear that glorious Word!

Refrain
Faith of our fathers, holy faith!
We will be true to thee till death.

In the case of Naboth, the vineyard was the "faith of our fathers." He described it as "the inheritance of my fathers." It belonged to generations in the past and generations in the future. It was an everlasting inheritance. It was an "unalienable right"—borrowing language from the U.S. Constitution—a right incapable of being repudiated, forfeited, or transferred to another. [9]

But there was still more to this vineyard. It represented more than Naboth's personal identity and more than his ancestral heritage. His loyalty to God also forbade the sale of the land.

3. The Vineyard Had to Do With His Spiritual Integrity

Again in verse 3 we read: "*The Lord forbid that* I should give the inheritance of my fathers to you!"

In other words, the land was a gift from God Himself to Naboth and his family. The Lord Himself had strictly forbidden this kind of transaction. The law of God was at stake, and this law was unchangeable. The land upon which Naboth had his vineyard was not for sale, because of his loyalty to God. Naboth's spiritual integrity forbade the sale of the property.

To help us understand where Naboth was coming from, how he viewed himself, his family, and the land, we could look in Leviticus 25:13-28, or Numbers 27:1-11; 36:1-13 (cf. Exodus 20:12). There we find that the concept of land given by God to the family is to be a perpetual gift for the family. For example:

> "The land shall not be sold permanently, for the land is Mine; for you are strangers and sojourners with Me....If one of your brethren becomes poor, and has sold some of his possession, and if his redeeming relative comes to redeem it, then he may redeem what his brother sold." (Leviticus 25:23,25)

> "So the inheritance of the children of Israel shall not change hands from tribe to tribe, for every one of the children of Israel shall keep the inheritance of the tribe of his fathers." (Numbers 36:7)

In simple terms, property in the ancient land of Israel couldn't be easily traded in the real estate market or stock exchange. It was viewed as a sacred inheritance. At least two important reasons existed for this law regarding land ownership:

1. God, in His divine wisdom, had set up this system to prevent the rich from hoarding the land and exploiting the poor. Even the lowliest servant should not lose the rights to his land. Property could only be transferred in extreme situations, and even in those circumstances, the land must return to its original owner in the year of Jubilee.

   Among other things, God wanted to protect the poor and the impoverished from unscrupulous developers and the like. His law ensured that every family, from the king down, could share the land. This is why, Naboth, a godly man with respect for God's law and trust in God's wisdom, had the nerve to stand up to the king.

2. God wanted to instill into the consciousness of all His people that He was and is the ultimate owner of all land. He has the title deed to all that we have—we are simply tenants or custodians. And if we're faithful stewards, He will one day give us a rich reward.

In other words, the land—or whatever we own today—is a little down payment of the heavenly kingdom God is preparing for us. And just as no one can take away the mansions He's prepared in heaven for us, so also no one should take away our apportioned lands. Thus, for Naboth to sell the vineyard would be to profane God's sacred gift. The vineyard had to do with his loyalty and integrity. And these obligations and qualities were also not for sale. The law of God which forbade the sale was grounded in the same authority of the One who spoke the Ten Commandments. And the Ten Commandments are not Ten Suggestions. Our Lord Himself said:

> "Do not think that I came to destroy the Law or the Prophets. I did not come to destroy but to fulfill. For assuredly, I say to you, till heaven and earth pass away, one jot or one tittle will by no means pass from the law till all is fulfilled. Whoever therefore breaks one of the least of these commandments, and teaches men so, shall be called least in the kingdom of heaven; but whoever does and teaches them, he shall be called great in the kingdom of heaven" (Matthew 5:17–19).

> "If you love me, keep my commandments" (John 14:15).

By the way, this is another reason why, in our morally relativistic culture, we must be suspicious of individuals who, in the name of "the gospel" or "grace," try to nullify the binding claims of the Law. God's Word declares:

> "Do we then make void the law through faith? God forbid: yea, we establish the law.... What then? Shall we sin, because we are not under the law, but under grace? God forbid....What shall we say then? Shall we continue in sin that grace may abound? Certainly not! How shall we who died to sin live any longer in it?" (Romans 3:31; 6:15, 1, 2).

Lovingly keeping His commandments, no matter what, is one of the identifying marks of God's end-time people: "Here is the patience of the saints; here are they who keep the commandments of God and have the faith of Jesus" (Revelation 14:12).

In short, a lot more was at stake in the seemingly harmless business proposal. (a) Naboth's identity, (b) his heritage—i.e., his family's history (past and future), and (c) his spiritual integrity and loyalty to God were tied to the land. It was for these reasons that land was not for sale.

4. Principled, But Courteous

No doubt Naboth was respectful with his answer, but he also meant what he said. He left no room for maneuver or negotiation. The land simply wasn't for sale. We can be sure that just as the king had given some four reasons as to why he had to have the land, Naboth also reiterated the same number of times why it was "Not for Sale."

This is how the king and Naboth might have negotiated in today's terms:

King Ahab: "Mr. Naboth, I need the vineyard for my vegetable garden."

Naboth: "I'm sorry, Mr. President, it's not for sale."

Ahab: "Mr. Naboth, as you know, the vineyard is near my house, and for aesthetic/landscaping and security reasons, I need to buy it."

Naboth: "I'm sorry, Sir, but I cannot trade in my civil liberties, constitutional right, or religious convictions in the name of homeland security. This is why this land is not for sale."

Ahab: "Well, Mr. Naboth, what if I exchange it for a better piece of land anywhere in my kingdom or even here in Jezreel? You have nothing to lose, but have everything to gain."

Naboth: "Sir, I'm very sorry, but this particular land is not for sale."

Ahab: "OK, Mr. Naboth, I'll pay you cash—an even better offer than the fair price—whatever you want for it."

Naboth: "Mr. President, I hate to disappointment you. But I don't want to give the impression that my refusal to give you the land is a gesture of disrespect to you as a person or to your office. Not at all, Sir. The reason I cannot sell it is because I am constrained by the law of God Almighty. The issue is more than a piece of real estate property. It is about loyalty to God and spiritual integrity. In simple terms, Mr. President, this ancestral land is not for sale, because it is a gift from God to me and my family, my ancestors before me, and my progeny after me. The gift is priceless, so there is no exchange that will be worth its sale."

Naboth is one of the unsung heroes of the Bible. He was faithful to God, even if it meant saying "no" to a powerful king. He would obey God rather than man. We need Naboths today—men and women who will not sell the truth for a loaf of bread, men and women who will not trade their integrity and morality for riches or popularity, men and women who will not barter biblical principle for political expediency, and men and women who will not compromise what is right because of fear of standing alone. *Naboth was one who could not be bought or sold.*

MEN WHO COULD BE BOUGHT AND SOLD

In contrast to Naboth, who could not be bought or sold, the Bible tells us that Ahab was a different kind of man. He was a man who *could* be bought and sold. In fact, the Bible describes Ahab in these words:

"But there was no one like Ahab who sold himself to do wickedness in the sight of the Lord, because Jezebel his wife stirred him up." (1 Kings 21:25)

He had sold himself to do wickedly. Elsewhere, the Bible records that "Ahab did more to provoke the Lord God of Israel to anger than all the kings of Israel who were before him" (1 Kings 16:33).

"Naturally of a covetous disposition, Ahab, strengthened and sustained in wrongdoing by Jezebel, had followed the dictates of his evil heart until he was fully controlled by the spirit of selfishness. He could brook no refusal of his wishes; the things he desired he felt should by right be his."[10]

Given Ahab's natural disposition to covetousness and selfishness, it was not surprising that he had sold himself to his queen, Jezebel. Let's see how the two partners reacted to Naboth's "not for sale" response, and the result of their action.

The Motive

King Ahab, described in verse 1 as "Ahab of Samaria," didn't view property the same way as did Naboth. Samaria, which was the home of Ahab's royal palace, was not an "ancestral inheritance" like Naboth's but a possession bought by his father, King Omri. Ahab's second home was in Jezreel, backing up to the coveted ancestral plot.

To Ahab, land was something one buys and possesses with money and with power. It was not tied to identity, ancestral heritage, or spiritual integrity. Thus, to Ahab, his offer to Naboth seemed a good deal—cash, or an even better vineyard. Who could refuse?

Yet, refuse Naboth did. And Ahab was frustrated. In fact, he was more than frustrated—he was depressed.

In verse 4 of our passage in 1 Kings 21 we see that human nature has not changed much throughout history. Apparently, pouting is not a new thing.

> "So Ahab went into his house sullen and displeased because of the word which Naboth the Jezreelite had spoken to him; for he had said, 'I will not give you the inheritance of my fathers.' And he lay down on his bed, and turned away his face, and would eat no food." (1 Kings 21:4)

Imagine the king of Israel, throwing a fit like a spoiled brat! Refusing to eat his peas because Naboth held on to his vineyard. Perhaps he even stuck out his jaw, or shed a few tears, before turning his face to the wall!

It is apparent that selfish people in positions of power cannot stomach the principled decisions of individuals who cannot be bought or sold. As in the days of Ahab, so in our day.

This is where another principal character comes into the picture—the woman to whom Ahab had sold himself. Given Ahab's covetous spirit, it didn't really matter who the new character was—male or female. But as we'd soon discover, his wife Jezebel was no ordinary personality.

The Mastermind

Jezebel was masterful, indomitable, implacable, a devout worshiper of Baal, and she hated anyone and everyone who spoke against or refused to worship her pagan god. She had earlier murdered many priests and prophets of God and caused others to go into hiding. In fact, at the time of this story, the prophet Elijah had been fleeing from Jezebel for about four or five years. Jezebel was the personification of malice, intrigue, wickedness, evil, and death. She enters the scene in 1 Kings 21:5, 6:

> "But Jezebel his wife came to him, and said to him, 'Why is your spirit so sullen that you eat no food?' He said to her, 'Because I spoke to Naboth the Jezreelite, and said to him, "Give me your vineyard for money; or else, if it pleases you, I will give you another vineyard for it." And he answered, "I will not give you my vineyard."'"

To Jezebel's credit, she apparently had a genuine concern for her husband, no matter how misguided her remedies for the situation turned out to be!

Perhaps I should mention, parenthetically, that the relationship between Ahab and Jezebel has a few lessons for how men and women relate today. It appears that men are increasingly behaving like immature boys—careless, irresponsible, and irresolute. Like Ahab, they cannot seem to exercise responsible leadership. As a consequence, our homes and churches face a crisis in leadership. Too many weak-kneed Ahabs are glued to their chairs and pews, abdicating their spiritual leadership responsibilities.

It's no wonder that the Eves of today are taking over many leadership roles! Reluctantly and of necessity, many women step into this vacuum to ensure the spiritual nurture of their children. Other women, like Jezebel, may be driven more by ambition to seize leadership roles. Yet even though Jezebel's motives for asserting leadership were selfish, her story is a rebuke to men even today who have abandoned their priestly roles—in both the home and the church.

As the sad story of Naboth's vineyard progresses, it becomes clear that Ahab is just as guilty as Jezebel. He begins by asking for something that wasn't Naboth's to give, then throwing a childish fit when he was refused. He then misrepresented Naboth to Jezebel, *conveniently "forgetting" to mention that there was a religious conviction behind the refusal.* Ahab's watered-down version of what happened didn't mention that Naboth's identity, his sense of ancestral inheritance, and his spiritual integrity stood in the way of the deal. This might not have stopped a woman like Jezebel, of course. But it might have given her pause. After all, she had seen three years of famine, fire fall out of the sky, and an incredible, heaven-sent deluge. She had seen 850 of her prophets and priests slain by the sword of the Lord (see 1 Kings 18). She was certainly aware of the power Israel's God could exercise when mere mortals—and even a headstrong queen—acted outside His counsel.

Instead, she saw exactly what Ahab represented the situation to be: a case of willful and even dangerous insubordination against "God's anointed leader" or a challenge of institutional authority or policy. To Jezebel, Naboth was an arrogant person who thought he was wiser than even the king and the collective decision of the royal advisors.

Being the shrewd and speedy decision-maker she was, Jezebel saw a simple—though totally unethical—solution to the problem immediately.

> ## "Then Jezebel his wife said to him, 'You now exercise authority over Israel! Arise, eat food, and let your heart be cheerful; I will give you the vineyard of Naboth the Jezreelite.'" (1 Kings 21:7)

Jezebel's response, "You now exercise authority over Israel!"—was a gentle rebuke. She seemed to be asking the king, "Who is in charge in Israel? Is it Naboth—or you? Do you now govern Israel?" (or, as the *New Living Translation* renders it, "Are you the king of Israel or not?")

The reply of Jezebel may have been rhetorical or sarcastic—but her actions spoke to what she valued. She exercised the royal rule that Ahab did not. She pronounced, in good royal manner, that she would get the vineyard for Ahab.

When Jezebel told the king, "I am going to get you that vineyard," we should not doubt her resolve or what she was likely to do. In fact, the Bible leaves us in no doubt:

"And she wrote letters in Ahab's name, sealed them with his seal, and sent the letters to the elders and the nobles who were dwelling in the city with Naboth. She wrote in the letters, saying, Proclaim a fast, and seat Naboth with high honor among the people; and seat two men, scoundrels, before him to bear witness against him, saying, 'You have blasphemed God and the king.' Then take him out, and stone him, that he may die." (1 Kings 21:8–10)

The Plot, Assassination, and Cover-up

No doubt Jezebel had henchmen who did her bidding—a highly trained hit-squad or "special forces" team that could take care of Naboth with a snap of a finger. Jezebel was too smart for that, however. Why risk a public relations fiasco for the king? Easier, more politically correct or even religious ways existed to accomplish her damnable deed.

So Jezebel, who may have been a writer of sorts, thought up a carefully worded memo. Then she penned her plan on parchment and sealed it with Ahab's own seal—the symbol of the legislative and executive authority invested in his office. She then sent the memo by priority mail to the nobles of Naboth's hometown.

"There's a need for renewal and transformation in the nation," she was saying. "Some great calamity or sin has been committed that threatens the security of our nation. We must humble ourselves and seek the face of the Lord." So she ordered the leaders of the city. The order she penned might have been as follows:

> "Declare a special national day of fasting and prayer. And let every citizen of Jezreel
> be present, both those who are spiritual (such as Naboth) and those who may not be
> considered so religious (such as the scoundrels—the sons of Belial [KVJ]). Be careful to
> include a special testimony service in the program. Who knows, at spiritual gatherings
> such as I propose, whether the Holy Spirit can so convict even non–church-goers that
> they may confess and give up their wicked ways. Of course, we also know that some—
> including so-called believers—may also harden their hearts and continue living in sin
> (cf. Ananias and Sapphira in the early church). Regardless of people's responses to the
> moving of the Spirit, on this national day of prayer and fasting, whoever is found blas-
> pheming God and the king—even if the culprit is a principled Naboth—they will face
> the full wrath of the law."

There's an irony in this sad account. Although Ahab left theology or God out of his vineyard deal when he reported it to Jezebel, the wicked queen used religion to carry out her plot to procure the vineyard for her husband.

Notice the shrewdness of the queen's strategy. By proclaiming a fast, she gave a religious twist—a non-threatening, peaceful veneer—to the whole sordid affair. She then arranged during the "testimony service" a mock and very fixed trial for Naboth, complete with false witnesses who apparently had no scruples, even in front of large crowds.

We can only faintly speculate on what happened on that national day of prayer and fasting— perhaps there was some inspirational music, a soul-searching sermon, an altar call and heartfelt prayers. Then came the time for the testimony service. I can see one young man—a well-known hardened criminal in town, stepping up to the microphone. With teary eyes and a voice filled with deep emotion, he begins:

> "I'm sure some of you are surprised that I'm standing before you today. But I'm here
> to testify of the power of God in transforming lives, even the lives of people like me—
> sons of Belial. I don't want to glorify Satan by recounting the things I used to do—many
> of you know them too well. I'm simply here to thank the Lord for saving my life. I'm
> also here to ask you all for forgiveness. Words are not enough to express my sorrow
> for the hurt I've caused many of you. Above all, I'm here to thank those of you who
> never gave up on me, but kept praying for me even when there was no sign that
> I would ever change.
>
> In a very special way, I want to thank the leaders of this church—and also our national
> leaders—for declaring this day of prayer of fasting. Perhaps I'm the sole reason for this
> day. By the grace of God I'm now born again, and I dedicate the remainder of my life
> to live for the Lord.
>
> I have only two words of admonishment to all of you: First, never give up on people like
> me: Though you classify us as "un-churched," many of us were really seeking for God,
> so never give up on any one. Second, those of you who claim to be principled Christians
> should be true to your convictions and start living lives worthy of your call. Some of
> you here are doing the very same things I used to do. In fact, you did it secretly with me.
> You know yourselves. My only prayer is that you will also take advantage of today and
> surrender all to Jesus. I would personally like to appeal to Mr. Naboth to also come clean
> before God and man—just as we have done..."

Can you imagine the utter shock of Naboth, when on this special day of spiritual revival, prayer, and fasting, this new believer then proceeded to accuse him of certain criminal acts and sinful lifestyle practices—even stating that Naboth had cursed God and the king? How could he, Naboth—a conscientious believer and loyal citizen—be accused of blasphemy and treason—two accusations that in those days called for the death penalty? How could he, who had honestly strived to keep the law, even against his king, be accused of committing a breach of the law by blaspheming God and the anointed of God?

The charges were so utterly ridiculous that Naboth might have thought that no one would believe them. After all, his neighbors knew him well from his youth as being an honest and upright man, and they were also familiar with the character of his accuser. But Naboth was mistaken. Another newly repentant citizen (who, until that national day of prayer, was also well-known to be a liar, gangster, and thief) also added his voice in silencing Naboth's protestations of his innocence. He too insisted that he had heard Naboth blaspheme God and the king!

Naboth was stunned and speechless—a fact that led the church members and all the leaders to assume his guilt. When he finally regained his composure and tried to express his innocence, the two former "un-churched" members expressed their outrage at his hypocrisy. They also denounced the hypocrisy in the church, especially that of the so-called religious conservatives and their ministers who condoned such actions. The former "seeker-sensitive" members explained that it was this kind of behavior, as exhibited in the life of Naboth, that had driven them—and many other young people—out of church in the first place. They threatened, "Unless the church does something about this situation, we will not be part of your religious system."

No way was left for Naboth to defend himself, for the "truth" was established by the agreement of the two witnesses. And since he had apparently hardened his heart against the pleadings of the Holy Spirit and the pleas of his fellow believers, he would be disfellowshiped from the church—which meant that he would be stoned immediately.

Before the day was over, the truth would lie cold with Naboth's bloody, mangled body under a pile of rocks. The biblical account simply reads:

> "So the men of his city, the elders and nobles who were inhabitants of his city, did as Jezebel had sent to them, as it was written in the letters which she had sent to them. They proclaimed a fast, and seated Naboth with high honor among the people. And two men, scoundrels, came in and sat before him; and the scoundrels witnessed against him, against Naboth, in the presence of the people, saying, 'Naboth has blasphemed God and the king!' Then they took him outside the city and stoned him with stones, so that he died." (1 Kings 21:11–13)

What might have gone through Naboth's mind, when he saw the unfolding of the plot—when the first blow of stones hit him and blood began streaming from his wounds? Perhaps he cried out to the Lord: "Oh, God, is this the reward for integrity? Is there no one to stand up in my defense and rescue me? Must I suffer this kind of shameful death? Where are you, God? Are you still on the throne? Why have you forsaken me?"

But there seemed to be no reply from his God. So Naboth—the man who couldn't be bought or sold—was murdered in cold blood on a "holy day" in the name of religion, so that Ahab could take possession of his vineyard.

But there's more to the sad story. According to the law, the king could only take possession of the property if the deceased in Israel had no heirs to inherit his possession. Unfortunately for Jezebel, Naboth had children. And as long as they were alive, Ahab couldn't just take Naboth's vineyard.

Jezebel would not let anything stand in her way. On receiving a text message on her iPhone about the children of Naboth, she quickly sent a reply, giving instructions on what should be done. A small detail in 2 Kings 9:26 completes the story: Naboth's innocent sons were also rounded up and murdered on that day! The Lord saw "the blood of Naboth and the blood of his sons."

Thus Naboth's property, left without heirs, reverted to the crown. It was a clean murder, nicely covered up, with no fingerprints of the real culprits. Ahab could now have the coveted vineyard.

"Then they sent to Jezebel, saying, 'Naboth has been stoned and is dead.' And it came to pass, when Jezebel heard that Naboth had been stoned and was dead, that Jezebel said to Ahab, 'Arise, take possession of the vineyard of Naboth the Jezreelite, which he refused to give you for money; for Naboth is not alive, but dead.' So it was, when Ahab heard that Naboth was dead, that Ahab got up and went down to take possession of the vineyard of Naboth the Jezreelite." (1 Kings 21:14, 15)

The tragic story of Naboth is one of the stories in the Bible from which one can draw a number of valuable lessons.

NOTES

6 1 Kings 16:29–34.

7 See Joshua, chapters 12–24.

8 Leviticus 25:13–28, or Numbers 27:1–11; 36:1–13.

9 The U.S. Constitution reads, in part: "We hold these truths to be self-evident, that all men are created equal, that they are endowed by their Creator with certain unalienable Rights, that among these are Life, Liberty and the pursuit of Happiness. That to secure these rights, Governments are instituted among Men, deriving their just Powers from the consent of the governed, — That whenever any Form of Government becomes destructive of these ends, it is the Right of the People to alter or to abolish it, and to institute new Government, laying its foundation on such principles and organizing its powers in such form, as to them shall seem most likely to effect their Safety and Happiness..."

10 E. G. White, Prophets and Kings, p. 204.

PART 2
MORE T
A STOR

Some S

Lessons

HAN
Y
obering

"To sin by silence when they should protest makes cowards of men."

Abraham Lincoln
16th U.S. President,
1809–1865

AN UNHOLY ALLIANCE

Due to a lack of knowledge of biblical teaching, some might have difficulty understanding why Naboth would turn down what seemed like an excellent business offer. They might view him as a "poor ignorant farmer, too stupid to take what was profitable." Otherwise, why would he turn down a good business deal for sentimental reasons?

Even if critics give Naboth credit for standing up for his rights or religious principles, they might still think that those are not things upon which one should risk one's life. At the very least, they would view Naboth as fanatical, if not a religious extremist.

But such an assessment of Naboth misses the bigger picture and the vital lessons from the story. His death represents the right of people to practice their faith and to stay true to their convictions. Furthermore, such an evaluation can even be dangerous, in that it can easily lead to religious intolerance and persecution—a fact amply documented in history.

Naboth was not being blind, foolish, or reckless. He knew the value of what he was turning down in Ahab's offer. He also had a full understanding of the importance of his beliefs, and he made a choice. He decided that his faith was more important than any amount of money or material wealth. He refused to "sell out." Ahab and Jezebel should have respected his decision, his fundamental right to make that choice, regardless of whether or not they agreed.

We should commend the Naboths who are true to their convictions, and challenge the Ahabs and Jezebels who resort to tyranny against the people with whom they disagree. In this context, the actions of Jezebel give a glimpse of what could happen again, on a much larger scale, in current history.

The context of this tyranny was the political marriage between Ahab and Jezebel—an unholy alliance that changed both religion and politics in Israel—and an action that earned Ahab the epithet as one who "did evil in the sight of the Lord, more than all who were before him." [11]

It is always dangerous when powerful religious forces, represented in this story by Jezebel, align themselves with political rulers of the land—symbolized by Ahab. When this situation occurs, it is almost inevitable that the religious forces will bring out the seal of Ahab—the legislative and executive powers of civil government—and use that seal to prosecute and persecute the Naboths who cannot be bought or sold.

While religion has played positive roles in transforming the politics of nations, history has also documented the negative outcome of religion in the political world. [12] Religion is a powerful tool to mobilize people because its seemingly divine authority has the power to convince when the government alone fails to do so. But religion's power can be dangerous, when abused for political agendas or purposes.

In this respect, Jezebel is not alone in misusing religion. This type of dangerous alliance that was used by Jezebel to pursue Ahab's covetous whim, has been used for larger and more recent atrocities. The Middle Ages, the Holocaust, apartheid, and the ongoing conflicts in the Middle East are only a few examples.

From Naboth's story, and from our lessons in history, we should beware of any power—religious or political—which tries to coerce us to give up our rights and to compromise the freedom of our fellow. We must also be aware of the dangers that can threaten the greater good of humanity when religion is used by covetous leaders and vice-versa. And we must make sure that we do not compromise our convictions of what is right because of pressure from "God or King."

It is never right to violate basic freedoms, even if it is in the name of the security of the government or the nation or the world, or even in the name of upholding or promoting religious values from God.

The experience of Naboth reveals the irrationality of religious persecution and the many forms under which it can take shape. It also highlights the times in which we live and the crisis that could follow if fear and religion are used to manipulate people or cause others to forfeit their rights and even their lives.

PULLING DOWN THE WALLS

I'm afraid that, already, in many countries, powerful religious and political coalitions are working with governments to legislate religious laws. In many lands, the healthy wall of separation between religion and politics, between church and state, is slowly being pulled down. This trend is discernible even in the United States—a nation that has historically maintained "a friendly separation of church state." [13]

Ahab and Jezebel are getting married.

Unless we learn from history, sooner or later, Jezebel will use Ahab's seal. She will falsely accuse the Naboths--men who will not be bought or sold, and men who stand for right and honor God--of blaspheming the very one who they worship. She will persecute the Naboths, accusing them of being threats to national security and of affronting religious values. The Naboths will die for their identity, heritage, and spiritual integrity, which would not bend to the political marriage between Ahab and Jezebel.

It is our choice. We can be principled Naboths, or we can be unscrupulous Ahabs and Jezebels. If we're not "men who will not be bought or sold," we shall be accomplices in the murder of some innocent Naboths.

ACCOMPLICES IN THE CRIME

Who sold Naboth to his death? Who would you single out as the most responsible for the shameful death of Naboth? If you were to point a finger at the people who killed Naboth, who would they be?

A close study of the account reveals that a number of people had blood on their hands. They are:

1. Ahab

The first accomplice on the list was the king himself, a weak-kneed and immature ruler. Undoubtedly, his natural tendencies toward covetousness was the real cause of Ahab's complicity in the cold-blooded murder.

Ahab had to have known exactly what Jezebel had in mind, when she had declared, "I will give you the vineyard of Naboth the Jezreelite." It wouldn't have taken a soothsayer or psychic to figure it out. The king might not have known the details. He might even have deceived himself into thinking that his intentional lack of knowledge absolved his guilt. But as we shall see later in the story, nothing was farther from the truth. Even if he was ignorant of her intentions, still the readiness with which he went forth to reap the fruits of her crime makes him an accomplice. Those who wittingly profit by others' wrongdoings should share in their condemnation too.

King Ahab had already sold himself to the wicked queen Jezebel. Like many men today, Ahab was a reckless and irresolute ruler—a man who had abdicated his God-ordained leadership responsibilities, in the home and in the church.

Yes, Ahab was the prime accomplice in the murder of Naboth. In fact, the Bible condemns him in these words:

> "But there was no one like Ahab who sold himself to do wickedness in the sight of the Lord, because Jezebel his wife stirred him up. And he behaved very abominably in following idols, according to all that the Amorites had done, whom the Lord had cast out before the children of Israel....Ahab did more to provoke the Lord God of Israel to anger than all the kings of Israel who were before him."
> (1 Kings 21:25, 26; 16:33)

But others were also active participants in the plot, murder, and cover-up.

2. Jezebel

I don't think anyone would doubt that Jezebel was the real mastermind of this criminal action. She was a wickedly unscrupulous woman. She was evil—a woman of consummate subtlety, duplicity, and cruelty.

Queen Jezebel was the daughter of Ethbaal, King of the Zidonians (1 Kings 16:31) and wife of Ahab, the King of Israel. As a king's daughter and a king's wife, she was used to power—and the abuse of power. Jezebel was more daring and reckless in her wickedness than was her wicked husband, whom she "stirred to do evil (v. 25). She was so wicked that in the New Testament book of Revelation, Jezebel is made a symbol of the end-time religious rebellion against God and His people. [14]

No one would deny that pointing a finger at Jezebel is to vilify her for being a self-promoting, overly ambitious woman. It is not sexism or male chauvinism to assign blame to this cold-blooded murderer. She was guilty. What made her crime more hideous is the fact that although she was the sworn enemy of the Law of God, she maliciously utilized the provisions of the divine law to plot and execute Naboth's death.

But to single out Jezebel or be fixated by her would be to miss the real injustice carried out by the others who had sold themselves to her to do evil.

3. Sons of Belial

Likewise, the involvement of the "sons of Belial" or scoundrels, should come as no surprise. As their very name shows, they're not on the side of good.

The phrase *sons of Belial* occurs frequently in the Old Testament. It is used to describe people who were "wicked," "lawless," "worthless" or "base fellows" (so also the "daughter of Belial"). [15] In the New Testament it is found only in 2 Corinthians 6:15, where it is used as a name of Satan, the embodiment of all that is evil.

In the story of Naboth's vineyard, the "sons of Belial" were the people who did the actual dirty work. Modern translations refer to them as "scoundrels"—people who behave dishonorably toward other people. They were liars, villains, and considered to be the scum of the earth. They were hit men, assassins, or mercenaries who would do anything with consciences unmoved. They were the kind that everyone knew would sell their souls for a cent or less.

Since these "sons of Belial" had already sold their consciences for money to hold them solely accountable would be to flog a dead horse. More important, it would deflect attention away from the many faceless individuals who are often overlooked in criminal conspiracies and behaviors.

4. The Unnamed Individuals

At this point it is necessary to call attention to the individuals whose hands drip with the blood of Naboth and who are seldom mentioned in criminal conspiracies. They are the individuals whose identities are often concealed under anonymity.

In verse 8 the Bible informs us that Jezebel addressed her memo to "*the elders and the nobles who were dwelling in the city with Naboth.*" Again in verse 11, we read that "*the men of his city, the elders and nobles who were inhabitants of his city*, did as Jezebel had sent to them, as it was written in the letters which she had sent to them."

Twice, the Bible states that the anonymous individuals who participated in the plot to murder Naboth were the elders, nobles, and citizens of the city.

Much of the remainder of this work will be devoted to these elders and nobles of Jezreel.

THE IDENTITY OF THE ELDERS AND NOBLES

Who were these men of Naboth's city—these elders and the nobles—who allowed their fellow citizen to be murdered?

They were the respected leaders of the city. If they lived in our day, we would easily recognize the "elders and nobles" as being the mayors, councilmen, congressmen, judges, and campaign managers of the political parties. They are the sheriffs and deputies in the police department, the scholars and teachers in the classrooms. They are the youthful and idealistic political activists on college and university campuses. They are the doctors, lawyers, journalists, engineers, bankers, and those who attend conventions of Christian business men and women. They are the pastors and leaders at various levels of church administration. They are the local church officers and laypersons of significant influence. They are the respected fathers and husbands in the homes. They are the student leaders in church institutions.

Today, we'll call these respectable elders and nobles "men of faith"—the Michigan men of faith![16]

These leaders—these civic, religious, business, community, and student leaders—were the ones who played along in Jezebel's intrigues to satisfy the insatiable covetousness of her irresponsible husband.

- They were the ones who were asked to declare a phony national day of prayer and fasting.

- They were the ones who were expected to employ some of the local street boys, gangsters, low-lifes, and mafia-style hit-men.

- They were the ones who concocted lies, fabricated evidence, and brought false accusations against their neighbor—they charged Naboth with blasphemy and treason.

- They were the ones who convened a kangaroo court, sat as judge and jury, passed judgment, and carried out the death sentence.

I will assert that the real criminals are not the Jezebels, Ahabs, or the sons of Belial. These are very easy to identify and blame. But the ones who need exposing, *the ones who deserve scorn and condemnation, are the ones who look very much like us*—the elders and nobles.

They are the people you know—the people who live next to you, attend the same school with you, work at the same place with you, and worship in the same church with you. In fact, they are your best friends, family members, and professional colleagues. And don't be surprised that you could even be one of them!

The elders and nobles of today's Jezreel are the otherwise well-meaning leaders of the community, city and church.

- They are the ones who tend to fear man more than God.

- They are the schemers, the ones who *go along to get along*.

- They are the ones who are unwilling to rock the boat, even when they know the boat is heading down the wrong stream.

- They are those who cowardly stand idly by as things go wrong in the church.

- They are the ones who remain silent when people ought to speak up.

- They are the people who like to be in the background while pulling the strings.

- They represent those who do their dirty work, without ever dirtying their own clean hands.

- They are the people who have more faith in the threatening fingers of the powerful establishment than in the arm of the Almighty.

- They are those who are just plain fearful and too cowardly to take a principled stand and face the consequences.

These nameless individuals need to be exposed for their criminal complicity. They need to be defined, so that we can recognize them and beware of their threat. They need to be revealed so that we can make sure we do not end up in their ranks. As in the days of Naboth—and our day—these elders and nobles of Jezreel were the ones most responsible for selling Naboth to his premature death.

Don't tell me that these individuals didn't know better. Don't tell me that they didn't understand the implications of their complicity and the outcome of their actions. Don't tell me that they were innocent. Don't tell me the "elders and nobles" were amateurs or novices.

No! A thousand times No! These were not ignorant. They knew well that what they were doing was wrong. They understood fully that they were sentencing a friend, neighbor, classmate, colleague, and church member to death. Still, they did it.

Not just one or two of them. Not just a small group of conspirators. No, it took all of them: the whole church leadership and administrators, the city councilmen, and the nation's congressmen and parliamentarians. It was a community farce and a communal lynching.

And among them were individuals who were otherwise good people—elders and nobles of the city. They were the church board members, the executive committee members, the leaders at higher levels of church administration, the delegates attending church conventions and conferences.

But even here, it is easy to apply the tragedy of Naboths death to individuals we already know to be responsible for the problems and ills in the church and the society.

Thus, it is easy to apply the passage to some corrupt, right-wing politicians or some zealous religious leaders—whether they be some extremist Muslim or Hindu fundamentalists or some Christian fundamentalists (in all their theological stripes, whether Roman Catholic, Protestant, Pentecostal/Charismatic, non-denominational, or even some radical independent Christian groups). We can even cite instances of their mean-spirited fanaticism, judgmentalism, and extremism. We can also point out cases of their pious hypocrisy and legalistic spirituality. Yes, we can even reference how their "narrow-minded" intellectual obscurantism has stifled legitimate innovation, advancement, and cooperation with people of other views. It is easy to look at these elders and nobles as overzealous religious extremists or homophobic bigots—a few "bad apples" in the tray of good religious people.

It is also easy to see these elders and nobles as representatives of the liberal thought leadership who seek to redefine the church and its mission. We can document how, in their bid to promote their "progressive" ideas, they seek to water down or even remove those beliefs and standards that "the world" might find even remotely objectionable. We are very much aware of how, at major gatherings of the church, they plan, vote, and legislate unbiblical practices in the church. We know what they are teaching in the classrooms, local churches, and in their published articles. We are familiar with how, on issues of feminism, gay rights, worship, and others, they seem far more concerned with being "politically correct" or producing a desired outcome, than with knowing, preaching, and practicing the clear Word of God on such matters. We are aware of how they push such agendas in carefully choreographed strategies in denominational publications, media programming, and church gatherings. We can attest to how they speak about "tolerance" and "inclusiveness," yet display no such graces toward those who challenge their questionable views. We can even show how, under their leadership, our churches and institutions have lost their sense of identity and mission, and how these churches and institutions have experienced stunted numerical and spiritual growth.

But it is far too easy to point our fingers to others. It is altogether very easy to apply the tragic story of Naboth's murder so that it's another sad account that is all about *them*—and to act as if it has nothing to do with *us*.

To do so, however, is to whitewash the enormity of the criminal act and to absolve ourselves of our complicity in it. To blame others, while failing to recognize *our* individual roles in the plot, is to miss the gravity of the murder of principled Naboth.

IT'S ALL ABOUT US

If we are really honest with ourselves, we know why we want to make the "elders and nobles of the city" a reference about them instead of us. We know that *at some profound and troubling level, it is about us.*

We are the people hidden behind the nameless group of elders and nobles.

- We know it is about *us* because we have employed the clout of our age, position, degrees, and money to silence the voice of truth and reform.

- We know it is about *us* because it describes our complicit involvement in that small intrigue or that white lie which is right now pinching our conscience.

- We know it is about *us* because there have been times when we have kept silent when we should have spoken up.

- We know it is about *us* because in our relationship with others we have consistently prized the unity of the group over the singularity of principle.

- We know it is about *us* because we have deliberately twisted the words and misrepresented the positions of others whose views differ from ours.

- We know it is about *us* because in reporting our side of accounts, our watered-down versions conveniently fail to mention the complete position of the people who disagree with us.

- We know it is about *us* because our inaction and our failure to correct deliberate misinformation at committee meetings have undermined the influence of those who are or could have been offering honorable service.

- We know it is about *us* because we have often remained quiet in the face of injustice, in order not to risk our standing and acceptance within our community and organization.

We were the elders and nobles who did not raise a voice to save the life of Naboth. We were the final court of appeal to have spared the life of that principled man. Even if one of us on that jury had spoken up, perhaps others would have joined in staying the murderous course. Yet none of us did anything. And by our silence we pronounced the death sentence upon an innocent man to satisfy our own selfish interests.

I say again: The account is not about them—whether conservative or liberal, religious or secular, or however else we draw the line between *us and them*. It is about *us*. We are part of the anonymous group of elders and nobles. We constitute a vital link in the conspiracy of silence.

- We know it is about *us* because of the many times we allowed ourselves to drift along with the tide of wrong and evil because it was very "uncomfortable" to move against the flow.

- We know it is about *us* because we have often preferred the comfort of tradition, feeling, and culture over painful road of biblical truth.

- We know it is about *us* because we are aware of instances in our own lives when we should have stood up for our neighbor, but instead have joined in throwing stones.

- We know it is about *us* because we have used people to do our dirty work, justifying our scheming with the platitude that it is better for one person to suffer injustice than risk the security of the majority.

- We know it is about *us* because, for fear of being held accountable, we have often chosen the path of willful ignorance or a lack of interest in what's going on.

- We know it is about *us* when we've pointed our finger at others knowing full well that the three pointing back at us were the ones pointing in the right direction.

- We know it is about *us* because when others trusted us as their last shield of protection we betrayed their trust by our cowardice.

How often has the life of the innocent been sacrificed through the silence of those of us who should have been guardians of justice!

We are the elders and nobles of the city. We could have saved Naboth. But we chose to do nothing about it, because it was not politically expedient. We should be held guilty of criminal behavior for yielding to the sin of silence and inaction and for squandering the opportunity to stay the tide of evil.

No, the biblical account is not about them but about us. It is we who chose to be indifferent and neutral when the cause of truth was at stake.

But inspired counsels make it abundantly clear that we commit a criminal act any time we remain silent in the face of injustice. The holy Scriptures declare that indifference and inaction with respect to the cause of God is viewed by Him as a crime and the worse type of hostility to God.

The criminal action of the elders and nobles of Jezreel was similar to the sin of Meroz, an Israelite town in Naphtali: "'Curse Meroz,' said the angel of the Lord, 'Curse its inhabitants bitterly, *Because they did not come to the help of the Lord, To the help of the Lord against the mighty*'" (Judges 5:23).

What had Meroz done? Nothing. The curse of God came upon them for what they had not done. And this was their sin. They came not up to the help of the Lord against the mighty. At the time when all were to show their colors, the men of Meroz chose to be gray or neutral.

The scandalous inaction of the elders and nobles also reminds us of the deafening silence of the vast majority of the people of Israel on Mount Carmel. When the prophet Elijah urged them to stop "halting between two opinions" and to declare their public stand either for God or Baal, not one in that vast assembly dared utter one word for God. The people were completely silent. They chose to remain neutral at the time of crisis (1 Kings 18:21). Christian author E. G. White refers to this incident and writes poignantly:

> "If God abhors one sin above another, of which His people are guilty, it is doing nothing in case of an emergency. Indifference and neutrality in a religious crisis is regarded of God as a grievous crime and equal to the very worst type of hostility against God."[17]

"Indifference and neutrality in a religious crisis is regarded of God as a grievous crime and equal to the very worst type of hostility against God."

Can we still doubt the fact that the reason we want to make the "elders and nobles of the city" a reference about *them* is that, deep down in our hearts, *we know it is about us*? It is about us—we who claim to be religious, Christians, and even loyal members of the church.

- We know it is about *us* because our voices of apathy are often louder than the courage of our convictions.

- We know it is about *us* because in our fear of appearing intolerant or unloving we have been hesitant, waffling, and ambiguous on biblical teachings and principle.

- We know it is about *us* because in the churches we attend, our silence and actions have encouraged many frivolities in worship, dress, and lifestyle.

- We know it is about *us* because we have sat quietly as unconverted and incompetent individuals have been appointed to spiritual leadership.

- We know it is about *us* because we have maliciously criticized or failed to support the efforts of those faithful ministers who are selflessly serving.

- We know it is about *us* because we have allowed some of our pastors and leaders to get away with so many questionable ideas and agendas they have pontificated from the pulpits.

- We know it is about *us* because in our denominational institutions we have failed to take action against any teachers, thought leaders, and administrators who are undermining the teachings and values they are paid to uphold.

- We know it is about *us* because in the classrooms of our secular campuses we've allowed certain illogical, inconsistent, and fallaciously dangerous ideas of our teachers and professors to go unchallenged.

- We know it is about *us* because, for fear of being branded controversial and divisive, some of us preach only bland, wishy-washy or insipid messages that lead no one to heart-searching and repentance.

- We know it is about *us* because, in order to protect our positions and benefits, we have allowed some unscrupulous church administrators and institutional leaders to get away with their lies and vindictive actions at committee meetings.

- We know it is about *us* because we have at times hidden behind "respect" for "the Lord's anointed," church structure, and policy to not hold elected and appointed leaders accountable to truth.

- We know it is about *us* because, out of laziness, willful ignorance, or arrogance, we sometimes have believed the questionable theology of indifference and neutrality, arguing that "we're neither for nor against" some disputed biblical truth.

Let's quit pretending that we don't know that it's about us. Deep down in our hearts we know the truth. And the verdict is equally plain: "Indifference and neutrality in a religious crisis is regarded of God as a grievous crime and equal to the very worst type of hostility against God."

WE ARE THE ONES!

Unless human nature has recently and radically changed, there are some who would be offended, even outraged, by the indictment that we are the elders and nobles of the city. They may even denounce the message and messenger for painting the problems of the church and society with too broad and forceful strokes of the brush.

With great dignity and righteous indignation—commensurate with their age, position, or standing—some would argue that things are not as bad as they've been described. I can even over-hear one such person piously saying to oneself: "I know that I'm not perfect; but I'm not as bad as I've been described. I cannot possibly do that which you are implying I'm doing."

How self-deceived we all can be! We can usually see, with crystal clarity the sins and faults in others. But we cannot seem to see the sin in our own lives!

To the one unwilling to admit his complicity and sin of silence, I'd borrow the language of Nathan the prophet and say *"thou art the man!"*[18]

How ironic that those of us who are guilty of a particular sin are often in denial, even as we are quick to see—and condemn—this sin in the lives of others. How sad and tragic that some of us would be offended that we are included among the elders and nobles.

Let's stop fooling ourselves. We are self-deceived when we think it is about them, and not about us. The criminal conspirators of the city of Jezreel are a reference to us—you and me, whether we profess religion or feign agnosticism or atheism.

At the risk of being stoned to death, let me be a little more specific in showing why the "elders and nobles" refers to us. I know you'd prefer that I stay at the level of generalities, and not be too specific. But as Martin Luther correctly noted:

> If I profess with the loudest voice and clearest exposition every position of the truth of God except precisely that little point which the world and the devil are at that moment attacking, I am not confessing Christ, however boldly I may be professing Christ. Where the battle rages, there the loyalty of the soldier is proved; and to be steady on all the battle field besides, is mere flight and disgrace if he flinches at that point.[19]

So, at this solemnly critical hour in the history of the world, permit me to be more specific in pointing out concerns about the haves and have-nots in society. On the eve of racially charged atmosphere in our political discourse and processes, allow me to mention the racial injustices and behaviors still inherent in the system, both in society and in churches.[20] Let me speak candidly about the situation that obtains even in certain quarters of my own church:

- *We* are the elders and nobles, whenever we have remained silent when there was opportunity for us to act nobly and courageously in treating people of all races and socio-economic backgrounds as equal.

- *We* are the elders and nobles, whenever we have shirked our responsibility to show concern for the poor, defenseless, weak, and oppressed, and instead we have blamed the innocent, vulnerable, and helpless for the injustices they suffer.

- *We* are the elders and nobles, whenever we have winked at unjust laws and policies and have wittingly profited from the guilt-gotten spoils of those unfair legislations or enactments.

- *We* are the elders and nobles, whenever, instead of competence and spirituality, we have allowed racism, cronyism, and other ideologies to determine eligibility for office or appointment.

- *We* are the elders and nobles, whenever, *behind closed doors*, we have used racial slurs, epithets and jokes for other races or have resorted to innocent caricatures and stereotypes to describe them.

- *We* are the elders and nobles, whenever, because of our will-to-power, we have exhibited covert political maneuvers at church council deliberations, elections, and appointments.

- *We* are the elders and nobles, whenever we have encouraged race flight in the churches when other races begin to worship with us.

- *We* are the elders and nobles, whenever, to get along with the opportunists of our race, we have gone along with the continued existence of racially segregated churches and institutions in North America.

Deep within our hearts, we know that these structures of racism—however reasonable they may have been in the past—are neither right nor valid today.[21] Our children and grandchildren know they're not right, and in their own ways are working to bring about racial harmony, reconciliation, unity, and integration. But we—perpetrators, beneficiaries, *and* victims of racism—pretend that nothing can be done about the situation. And we choose to be comfortable with our racism.

- *We* are the elders and nobles, whenever we mirror the prejudice we ourselves have experienced and retaliate with prejudice, bitterness, and anger.

- *We* are the elders and nobles, whenever we get suspicious of the intentions behind all genuine gestures of goodwill from persons belonging to the other race, and we erroneously rebuff those gestures as hypocritical.

- *We* are the elders and nobles, whenever we accuse and blame the children of the other race for the wrongs committed by their parents and grandparents.

- *We* are the elders and nobles, whenever we cast every conflict between us and others as a racial problem, and blame the results of our own lack of responsibility upon other races.

- *We* are the elders and nobles, whenever we have celebrated their histories as monuments to tokenism, and not because the other races' experiences have kinship with our own.

- *We* are the elders and nobles, whenever we fail to see the inconsistency of embracing the other races as our brothers and sisters *in Christ*, but never as our brothers—and sisters-*in-law*.[22]

I've been speaking rather candidly about the forbidden issue of racism *and* the structures of racism within certain quarters of the church in North America. Why should our practice today be in marked contrast to the biblical example of our leading pioneers, several of who had at an earlier time identified with the Abolitionist movement—a minority movement in the USA opposing slavery?[23] Why cannot we be as courageous as other members of our church who later contributed to the Civil Rights movement in North America?[24]

Unfortunately, today, whoever dares to challenge the myths on racially separate church structure is likely to incur the wrath of advocates—both Black and White. Against this culture of silence, we need men and women who will refuse to be comfortable with the *status quo*. We must echo the words of E. G. White, one of our leading pioneers, and say:[25]

> "I know that which I now speak will bring me into conflict. This I do not covet, for the conflict has seemed to be continuous of late years; but I do not mean to live a coward or die a coward, leaving my work undone. I must follow in my Master's footsteps."[26]

But the examples highlighted above are not limited to just one nation. Variations can be found in almost every culture where one group of human beings is considered inherently inferior or less human.[27] And when we keep silent, as we often do, when the latter group is exploited, unfairly treated, or even abused, we are repeating the criminal conduct of those who were involved in the death of Naboth. So I say again that:

- *We* are the elders and nobles, whenever we masquerade our contempt for some races and nationalities by acting as if the church of the West is more principled, enlightened, or mature than the rest of the world church.

- *We* are the elders and nobles, whenever we display our cultural snobbery and arrogance by blackmailing, defying, or circumventing the theological consensus of the worldwide church on issues of faith and practice.

- *We* are the elders and nobles, whenever we have placed prejudicial stumbling blocks in the path of our children and have sometimes allowed them to mimic our racial attitudes and actions.

- *We* are the elders and nobles, whenever we have tried to use our money and names to buy positions or legislate our agendas.

- *We* are the elders and nobles, whenever, in board or committee meetings, we have remained silent when we should have spoken up.

- *We* are the elders and nobles, whenever, in the church, we have found convenient religious justifications to push biblically questionable ideologies and agendas of certain political systems or parties.

- *We* are the elders and nobles, whenever our lack of integrity makes us wait until retirement before declaring or articulating our true theological views.

- *We* are the elders and nobles, whenever, although we have the power and resources to make a difference in the lives of young people and secular university and college students, we choose to be indifferent.

We, the elders and the nobles of the city, are the ones responsible. It is we who have perhaps too often been bought and sold by the powers that be—whether political or ecclesiastical. It is we who have—whenever we've done so—murdered righteous Naboth. It is we who have stood idly by as Naboth's children were lynched. We are the ones who have blood on our hands.

> "For your hands are defiled with blood,
>   And your fingers with iniquity;
>   Your lips have spoken lies,
>   Your tongue has muttered perversity."
> (Isaiah 59:3)

And in the words of Martin Luther King, Jr., "We will have to repent in this generation not merely for the vitriolic words and actions of the bad people, but for the appalling silence of the good people."

NOTES

11 1 Kings 16:29-34.

12 Throughout history, religion has played a paradoxical role in various aspects of human society. For example, though preoccupied with the reality of the world which cannot be seen (God, angels, spirits, heaven, etc.), religion has been involved in the mundane details of everyday life (agriculture, farming, death, puberty, etc.). Religion has given rise to the most lofty human ideals, but it has also been used to justify the most extreme forms of cruelty. Whereas religion has often conjured up moods of the most sublime exaltation, it has also evoked images of dread and terror. Because of religion, new trails have been blazed into the heart of the unknown (such as scientific advancement) and utopias have been founded in its name (one can think of Calvin's Geneva and Ayatollah's Iran). And yet, religion has also served to bind upon the backs of people outworn shackles of custom or belief. Through common worship and other symbols of religion human groups have been united in the closest ties known to humanity. Yet religious differences have helped to account for some of the fiercest group antagonisms. Religion has also promoted harmony, as well as social conflict: In the name of religion many have advocated non-violence and peace, yet in the same name some have taken arms to kill. And religion has not only brought people together, it has also assigned people to different and unequal statuses (e.g., racism in apartheid South Africa, Hindu caste systems). See the classic work by Elizabeth K. Nottingham, *Religion and Society* (New York: Random House, 1954), pp. 1-11.

13 Church historian C. Mervyn Maxwell employs the phrase, "friendly separation of church and state" to describe the uniqueness of the American political experiment. Commenting on the First Amendment of the U.S. Constitution—"Congress shall make no law respecting an establishment of religion, or prohibiting the free exercise thereof"—Maxwell writes: "The grandest achievement of the American Constitution was the creation of a nation with a friendly separation of church and state. The world had never seen such a thing before. Every other nation since ancient times had taxed the people to support a state religion, and most had oppressed religious dissidents. The French Revolution, a little later than the American, experimented with a hostile separation of church and state. Marxist countries have exceeded France's temporary example. But America, with its friendly separation of church and state, salaried no clergy and taxed no congregation. She permitted denominations to proliferate and supported none of them. Her Congress said, 'In God we trust,' but elected not to define whether He is the God of Christians—or of Hindus." See C. Mervyn Maxwell, *God Cares: Volume 2, The Message of Revelation for You and Your Family* (Boise, Idaho: Pacific Press, 1985), p. 343.

14 See Revelation, chapter 2:18-29.

15 References to "sons of Belial" can be found in Deuteronomy 13:13; Judges 19:22; 20:13; 1 Samuel 1:16; 2:12; 10:27; 25:17, 25; 30:22; 2 Samuel 16:7; 20:1; 1 Kings 21:10, 13; 2 Chronicles 13:7; 6:15. The related expression "daughter of Belial" is found in 1 Samuel 1:16.

16 As explained in the Introduction, the first occasion of this presentation was at the Michigan Men of Faith convocation. The event took place on September 20, 2008, at the Great Lakes Adventist Academy, Cedar Lake, Michigan.

17 E. G. White, *Testimonies*, vol. 3, p. 281.

18 The phrase comes from 2 Samuel 12:7, where Nathan confronts King David for his adultery and complicity in the death of Uriah, a loyal soldier of the king, in order to marry his wife Bathsheba, who was pregnant with David's child. When attempts failed to make it appear that Uriah was the father of the child that his wife was expecting, David resorted to making her a widow so that he could take her as his own wife. Incredibly, Uriah was even used to deliver his own death warrant (2 Samuel 11:6-17). David thought that he could get away with it. He didn't. The Lord sent Nathan to David with a parable about a rich man who would not take from his own flocks and herds to feed a traveler on his journey, but took from a poor man his one little ewe lamb which he dearly loved. When David was angry and said that the man who had done this thing should die, Nathan answered, "Thou art the man."

19 I am indebted to the Internet website *http://www.gospelcom.net/cquod/cquodlist.htm* for the above quote. Each day this Christian website provides a noteworthy quotation for reflection. The above statement was posted on the site on May 1, 1997. I have yet to track down successfully the exact source reference in Luther's writings.

20 Race (from which the word *racism* is derived) is one great catchword that means different things to different people, and about which much ink and blood have been spilled. Despite this fact, no agreement seems to exist regarding what is a race, how it can be recognized, who constitute the several races, and how the different races are to be ranked in their relative abilities and closeness to some ideal referent (whether an ape, or a Creator). Thus, over the years, in an effort to abstract some defining traits as characteristic of a race, notable individuals—statesmen, scholars, scientists, etc.—have erroneously pointed to certain easily noted human features (such as color of the skin, hair, or eyes; the striking appearance of face or body; the unaccustomed mode of speech, language, dress, or religion; the shape of the skull; an unusual temperament, etc.) as the permanent, ineradicable hallmark of a race. For a critique of some of the different definitions of race, see Jacques Barzun's *Race: A Study in Superstition*, revised, with a new preface (New York: Harper & Row, 1965). Barzun argues that the idea of race is a fiction (not a fact), a "fatal superstition" that has been put forward from time to time to advance some ideological goal; see also Ashley Montagu, *Race Science and Humanity* (New York: Van Nostrand Co., 1963).

21 For a detailed discussion of racism and racially segregated structures within my own church in North America, see Samuel Koranteng-Pipim, *Must We Be Silent: Issues Dividing Our Church* (Ann Arbor, Michigan: Berean Books, 2001), pp. 299-441. This work deals with such divisive issues as homosexuality, women's ordination, church racism, liberalism's approach to the Bible, pluralism, gospel gimmicks, new worship styles, and General Conference session decisions.

22 Those contemplating interracial marriage need to be aware of some of the problems and pressures experienced by couples and children of interracial marriages. These factors add to the stresses commonly experienced in marriage. In most parts of the world, such factors make interracial marriages inadvisable at best and impossible to recommend. My concern here, however, probes the racial attitude that frowns on interracial/intertribal marriage or adoption for the *wrong* reasons, such as assuming that (1) some races are inherently inferior, or (2) intermarriage results in "blood mixing" or "mongrelization," or that (3) it is a case of spiritual "unequal yoking together." Such assumptions lead to the faulty conclusion that it is wrong or sinful for converted, Christian believers of different tribes or races to be married. Too often this conclusion results in their rejection and isolation. Is it possible that some of our opposition to interracial marriages has more to do with our own racial biases than with any kind of incompatibility (be it of religion, age, social status, ethnicity, etc.) that is likely to adversely affect the couple and the children who are involved in the marriage relationship? This question calls for honest searching of heart.

23 A number of our leading Seventh-day Adventist pioneers had at an earlier time identified with the abolitionist movement—a minority movement in the USA opposing slavery. Among these were: Joseph Bates (1792-1872), the former sea captain who did much to convince the early Adventists of the Sabbath truth; John Preston Kellogg (1807–1881), who harbored fleeing slaves on his Michigan farm and was the father of Dr. John Harvey Kellogg (the famous surgeon, inventor of surgical instruments, and resident physician at the Battle Creek Sanitarium); William K. Kellogg (the cornflakes manufacturer); and John Byington (1798–1887), pioneer minister and the first president of the General Conference of Seventh-day Adventists, who had maintained a station of the Underground Railroad at his home in Buck's Bridge, New York, illegally transporting slaves from the South to Canada. Some of the early Adventists were also closely associated with Sojourner Truth (c. 1797–1883), the itinerant anti-slave lecturer. Sojourner Truth, one of the Black heroes of abolition, was closely associated with the SDA work in Battle Creek. This itinerant lecturer against slavery enjoyed the friendship of John Byington, Dr. J. H. Kellogg, and other prominent SDAs. Not only did she regularly attend the Battle Creek Tabernacle church and camp meetings, but many students of Battle Creek College visited her home near Battle Creek regularly. In fact, one of her books was printed by the Adventist publishing house. The early Adventists were also closely associated with Frederick Douglas, a distinguished abolitionist who was attracted to the faith; though he never joined the church, his daughter became an Adventist. The fact that leading Adventist figures had previously been abolitionists undoubtedly influenced the attitude of the early SDA church on the question of the relationship between Blacks and Whites. For a sympathetic discussion, see F. D. Nichol, *The Midnight Cry* (Washington, D.C.: Review and Herald, 1944), 54, 175-178, 301; Roy Branson, "Ellen G. White: Racist or Champion of Equality?" *Review*, April 9, 1970, 3; Ronald D. Graybill, "The Abolistionist-Millerite Connection," in Ronald L. Numbers and Jonathan M. Butler, eds., *The Disappointment: Millerism and Millenarianism in the Nineteenth Century* (Bloomington, IN: Indiana University Press, 1987), 139-152; Louis B. Reynolds, *We Have Tomorrow: The Story of American Seventh-day Adventists With an African Heritage* (Hagerstown, MD: Review and Herald, 1984), 22-27. For an alternate assessment, see Malcolm Bull and Keith Lockhart, *Seeking A Sanctuary: Seventh-day Adventism and the American Dream* (San Francisco: Harper and Row, 1989), 194-197.

24 For example, author Jack Rummel, writing of the Adventist background of black leader Malcolm X, describes the Seventh-day Adventist Church as "one of the few mainly white religious groups that ignored America's color line" (see his *Malcolm X* [New York: Chelsea House Publishers, 1989], p. 25). Civil rights veteran Dorothy Height, in her autobiography, speaks of an incident in 1943 when she and fellow activists needed a gathering place in Tennessee, who in the end "proceeded to the Seventh-day Adventist College— one of the few local places that would allow an interracial meeting." See Dorothy Height, *Open Wide the Freedom Gates: A Memoir* (New York: Public Affairs/Perseus Books Group, 2005), p. 106. Such descriptions of Adventist practice, coming from outside observers and recalling a time in which integrated gatherings could bring violence and death, offer a noble tribute to our witness as a people.

25 Ellen G. White (1827–1915), an American, was a founding member of the Seventh-day Adventist (SDA) denomination. During her lifetime, when various Christian denominations in America were split over the thorny issues of slavery and Black and White racism, her stirring messages kept the Seventh-day Adventist church united. She led the SDA church to confront some of the major events in the area of race relations in United States—slavery, the civil war (1861–1865), the Emancipation Proclamation (1862), and the Reconstruction. As the church struggled with the issues of slavery, racial prejudice and discrimination, segregation, and its evangelistic and humanitarian responsibility in the South, she provided a prophetic voice. For a summary discussion of E. G. White's view on the Black-White racial situation in her day, see my *Must We Be Silent: Issue Dividing Our Church* (Ann Arbor, MI: Berean Books, 2001), pp. 353-413.

26 See her *The Southern Work*, p.10. It is not without significance that Mrs. White. made this statement in the context of race relations in America. She was not silent; neither must we. Because E.G. White traveled very widely–to England, France, Germany, Italy, Denmark, Norway, Sweden, and Australia–her perspectives on the Black and White relations in America also offer directions to Adventists today on how they should deal with racism in its various manifestations—tribalism, anti-semitism, anti-Arabism, anti-Islamism, etc.

27 Historically, the groups that have been treated as inferior or subhuman and possessing lives of little personal or societal worth have included people of color, Jews, native Americans, and Gypsies. Other groups, such as women, prisoners, the chronically ill, the physically disabled, the mentally retarded, children, the elderly, and unwanted babies, have also frequently been despised, denigrated, and dehumanized. Today, however, racism manifests itself in a baffling complexity, intensity, and respectability. Recent expressions of racism include (1) the tribal genocide in Rwanda, (2) the experiment of ethnic cleansing in Bosnia, (3) the practice, prevalent in some countries, of exploitation, domination, and abuse of defenseless children, women, and the physically or economically disadvantaged, because these forms of slavery enhance the quality of life of the superior race, 4) the countless cases of brutality, war, executions, abortions, euthanasia, etc., which are currently being carried out in different places because such acts of violence will make the world safer and better for the superior race. Though in America the word racism usually denotes conflict between white and black, this is much too narrow a definition. I have seen racism far stronger in Africa, where one tribe in an area or country seeks dominance over another. I have seen it in the Middle East, where the sons of Abraham still fight one another. I have seen it in various countries of Europe in the rise of ultranationalism and neo-Naziism. I have seen it in Canada, where differences in language and culture have fueled hostility among citizens of the same country. I have seen it in the former Soviet Union, where the fallen colossus seems destined to break into ever smaller warring pieces. And I have seen it in Asia, where religious and ethnic differences have ignited flames of violence. And in a post-9/11 world, where there is "war on terrorism," racism is sometimes manifest in anti-Arabism and anti-Islamism. Nor is the phenomenon limited to ethnic or nationalistic concerns. It may be seen in chauvinism of either gender, in the designation of an unborn child by the neutral term "fetus," so that it may be the more easily disposed of, and in the invisibility of people with various handicaps with which we prefer not to deal. No matter what lines we draw to elevate one group and denigrate another, we are dealing with the same issue.

PART 3
HEART
THE ST

Issues D
ing Ans

OF

ORY

emand-

vers

"In the end, we will remember not the words of our enemies, but the silence of our friends."

Martin Luther King Jr.
American Civil Rights Leader, 1929–1968

THEIR BLOOD CRIES OUT

The story of Naboth's vineyard brings up one of life's more difficult questions. Why do good people, like Naboth, sometimes suffer and die, while the wicked Jezebels, Ahabs, sons of Belial, and the "elders and nobles" live on, apparently unpunished?

Where was God when Naboth was killed? Was He even remotely nearby when His servant was wrongly accused? And where is God today when evil apparently triumphs? Where is God? Is He blind, that He cannot see? Is He deaf, that He cannot hear? Is He dumb, that He cannot speak? Is He paralyzed, that He cannot move? Where is God?

These questions often perplex faithful Naboths who are suffering unjustly. These questions were heard in the cries of brave martyrs.

Though the full answers to these questions may never be given in this life, of two facts we can be sure: God still sits on His throne, and all things work together for good for to them that love the Lord.

It's true that sometimes, for whatever reason, God's followers are allowed to suffer. History's pages are tainted by the blood of the innocent, from the blood of Abel; to the blood of Zechariah who perished between the altar and the temple in the Old Testament times (Luke 11:51); to the blood of John the Baptist, Stephen, James, Peter, and Paul in the New Testament.

Also, from the early church, on through medieval and Reformation times, all the way to the recent past and present centuries, innocent victims whose blood has been shed are too numerous to mention. And at the very end of time, the cries "of those who had been slain for the word of God and for the testimony which they held" (Revelation 6:9; cf. 12:17) will be heard—people like Naboth, who did not deserve to die.

When we stand face to face with injustice, it's important for us, as Naboths, to remember that one day, right will prevail. We live in a land of sin, but we still serve a God of justice. It may take awhile to arrive, but finally, Jezebel will have her day. Although no promise of justice exists here on this earth, God still reigns from the heavens. And God is still fair, though life is very unfair.

When it seems as if justice is fallen in the streets, when human verdicts are bought and sold, a God of the universe still keeps a tally of such things—a God who will vindicate His own. He will right all wrongs when He comes again, if not before. The great God of the universe sees all that happens on earth today, and He saw what happened to Naboth.

As God took action in the case of righteous Abel, so will He act again one day. He will confront our otherwise respectable brothers—the elders and nobles—who have hurt us. He will certainly take action, for He says: "The voice of your brother's blood cries out to Me from the ground" (Genesis 4:10).

We know justice will ultimately prevail, because it did so with the principal architects of Naboth's murder. God raised up a man of faith to confront Ahab and Jezebel:

"And it came to pass, when Jezebel heard that Naboth had been stoned and was dead, that Jezebel said to Ahab, 'Arise, take possession of the vineyard of Naboth the Jezreelite, which he refused to give you for money; for Naboth is not alive, but dead.' So it was, when Ahab heard that Naboth was dead, that Ahab got up and went down to take possession of the vineyard of Naboth the Jezreelite. Then the word of the Lord came to Elijah the Tishbite, saying, 'Arise, go down to meet Ahab king of Israel, who lives in Samaria. There he is, in the vineyard of Naboth, where he has gone down to take possession of it.'" (1 Kings 21:15–18)

THE GREAT CONFRONTATION

King Ahab wasn't always a man of inaction. When it came to taking over Naboth's much-wanted vineyard, he didn't let any grass grow under his feet. As soon as he knew that Naboth was murdered, Ahab went down to stake his claim.

But instead of meeting a real estate broker to sign the relevant documents of his new portfolio of farm holdings, he met someone else—a messenger from the real Owner of the land. And the meeting wasn't to seal a business deal, but rather to be served with his death warrant.

Elijah was an old acquaintance of Ahab. He had confronted Ahab on at least three previous occasions. He first confronted the king in Samaria, when the prophet announced the impending drought in Israel. Elijah later met him at the end of the three and half years of famine, when God summoned the prophet to go and show himself to Ahab. The last time Elijah confronted Ahab was on Mt. Carmel, in the presence of the 450 priests and 400 prophets of Baal, when Elijah called Ahab to stop halting between two opinions (see 1 Kings 17 and 18).

And now, after some four or five years of fleeing from the wicked king and his wife Jezebel, Elijah was commissioned once again by the Lord "to meet" Ahab. This meeting was going to be a great confrontation, for Elijah was going to deliver a message of judgment to the murderer of Naboth:

"Then the word of the Lord came to Elijah the Tishbite, saying, 'Arise, go down to meet Ahab king of Israel, who lives in Samaria. There he is, in the vineyard of Naboth, where he has gone down to take possession of it. You shall speak to him, saying, "Thus says the Lord: 'Have you murdered and also taken possession?'And you shall speak to him, saying, 'Thus says the Lord: "In the place where dogs licked the blood of Naboth, dogs shall lick your blood, even yours."'"
(1 Kings 21:17–19)

Elijah was not afraid to confront the king. He delivered the straight message the Lord had given him: "You murdered an innocent man and stole his property," the prophet said sternly. "Because of your sin, you will die."

"What?" Ahab may have made some vain attempt at explaining his rationale. "How could I have known what the queen would do?" he may have asked, lamely.

But the Lord knew the man who was really behind the murder. And God, who sees the thoughts and intents of the heart, is also aware of all plotters today. There are ways to tell lies without opening one's mouth; ways to steal without putting your hand in a pocket. God knows the truth. Whenever we are complacent or help someone commit a crime, we are guilty. So the Word still comes to us today. "Hast thou killed?" God wants to know.

- When we neglect the needs of the poor, Gods asks "Hast thou killed?"

- When we bear false witness against our neighbors, "Hast thou killed?"

- When mothers and parents don't provide healthy and balanced food for their children, God asks "Hast thou killed?" (Many graves should bear the epitaph, "Died because of poor cooking.")

- When, knowing what we know, we go on using drugs, alcohol, and other harmful narcotics, God asks "Hast thou killed?"

- When a young man or young woman are found at an abortion clinic, God asks "Hast thou killed?"

- When Bible-believing, commandment-keeping, pro-life Christians enlist as combatants in the wars of their tribes and nations, God asks "Hast thou killed?"

- When we overwork ourselves, trying to make more so we can spend more, God asks "Hast thou killed?"

- When we are tempted to think we can eat or drink anything we want, God asks "Hast thou killed?" Our bodies are the temple of God. We were bought with a price, and the Lord expects us to take good care of our health.

- When we cherish anger, vindictiveness, and an unforgiving spirit in our hearts, God asks "Hast thou killed?"

- When we bear false witness to ruin the reputation of others for our temporary gain, God asks "Hast thou killed?"

The sixth commandment—"thou shall not kill"—is far more encompassing than many realize:

> "All acts of injustice that tend to shorten life; the spirit of hatred and revenge, or the indulgence of any passion that leads to injurious acts toward others, or causes us even to wish them harm (for 'whosoever hateth his brother is a murderer'); a selfish neglect of caring for the needy or suffering; all self-indulgence or unnecessary deprivation or excessive labor that tends to injure health—all these are, to a greater or less degree, violations of the sixth commandment."[28]

When Elijah confronted Ahab—and us—with the rhetorical question, "Hast thou killed?" he was, in effect, declaring that although we may be successful in covering our role in killing others (and ourselves), one of these days our complicity will come out.

Whether we know it or not, God's holy angels are accurately detailing the biographical accounts of our lives. The Bible makes it abundantly clear that there is a record of the secret things we have done, including both our good and evil thoughts and words.[29] Writes my favorite Christian author:

> "Opposite each name in the books of heaven is entered with terrible exactness every wrong word, every selfish act, every unfulfilled duty, and every secret sin, with every artful dissembling. Heaven-sent warnings or reproofs neglected, wasted moments, un-improved opportunities, the influence exerted for good or for evil, with its far-reaching results, all are chronicled by the recording angel....

> "Sins that have not been repented of and forsaken will not be pardoned and blotted out of the books of record, but will stand to witness against the sinner in the day of God. He may have committed his evil deeds in the light of day or in the darkness of night; but they were open and manifest before Him with whom we have to do. Angels of God witnessed each sin and registered it in the unerring records. Sin may be concealed, denied, covered up from father, mother, wife, children, and associates; no one but the guilty actors may cherish the least suspicion of the wrong; but it is laid bare before the intelligences of heaven.

> "The darkness of the darkest night, the secrecy of all deceptive arts, is not sufficient to veil one thought from the knowledge of the Eternal. God has an exact record of every unjust account and every unfair dealing. He is not deceived by appearances of piety. He makes no mistakes in His estimation of character. Men may be deceived by those who are corrupt in heart, but God pierces all disguises and reads the inner life.

> "How solemn is the thought! Day after day, passing into eternity, bears its burden of records for the books of heaven. Words once spoken, deeds once done, can never be recalled. Angels have registered both the good and the evil. The mightiest conqueror upon the earth cannot call back the record of even a single day. Our acts, our words, even our most secret motives, all have their weight in deciding our destiny for weal or woe. Though they may be forgotten by us, they will bear their testimony to justify or condemn."[30]

Someday our Lord will judge us, even as He judged Ahab and Jezebel. And it was a grim future indeed that Ahab and Jezebel faced. Ahab would die, not in the comfort of a kingly palace, but in the very same spot where Naboth had bled. Jezebel would meet her fate also, and the dogs would lick her blood. These aren't some of the prettier prophecies in the Bible, but they were fulfilled—just as God said.

OUR FRIENDS OR OUR FOES?

Elijah became a messenger on a mission—a prophet with purpose. Ahab was not expecting to see Elijah! Perhaps he thought Elijah was dead—or that Elijah would be afraid to come back, after running away from the queen. But here now was the prophet again, standing before the king with a message of judgment.

Ahab must have felt like a child caught with his hand in the cookie jar. He knew he was guilty and that the reproving voice of the prophet was convicting. All Ahab could say was to accuse Elijah of being his foe: "Ahab said to Elijah, 'Have you found me, O my enemy?'" (verse 20).

It should come as no surprise that Ahab labeled Elijah as his "enemy," for wrongdoers always see right-doers as their foes. Like wicked Ahab, their lives are rebuked by the right.

This was not the first time Ahab had accosted Elijah and accused him of being a foe. Some three and half years after the prophet had prophesied about the impending judgment of a devastating drought, God sent him to summon Ahab and his false religious leaders to Mt. Carmel. At that encounter, Ahab accused Elijah: "Is that you, O troubler of Israel?"—to which Elijah responded firmly: "I have not troubled Israel, but you and your father's house have, in that you have forsaken the commandments of the Lord and have followed the Baals" (1 Kings 18:17, 18).

And now, more than four years after the showdown on Mt. Carmel, Ahab accused Elijah of being an "enemy," after being confronted by the prophet for his part in the murder of Naboth.

Ahabs always view Elijahs as trouble-makers and enemies. Because truth and messages that are singular are often perceived as negative, Ahabs do not consider faithful messengers as good "team players." Hence, in a culture of theological pluralism, those who stand for principle and sound biblical teaching are often branded controversial and divisive.

The truth, however, is that Elijah didn't come as Ahab's enemy—he came as his friend. Though the message he delivered was not pleasant, he dared to present it, when no one else was willing to do so. And speaking the truth in love, although seldom easy, is never the action of an enemy.

The Bible says, "Faithful are the wounds of a friend, but the kisses of an enemy *are* deceitful" (Proverbs 27:6). There is such a thing as friendly wounds, and there is also such a thing as wounding kisses. Sometimes when people kiss us and flatter us, it's not because they love us. Rather, it is a sign that they don't care about us. It takes a true friend to tell us what we need to hear, even if we don't want to hear it.

Yet how often we turn our best friends into enemies, as Ahab did Elijah. Neither Jezebel, the sons of Belial, nor the elders and nobles of Jezreel were the friends of Ahab. For they all aided him to do wrong. They did not say a word when Naboth was set up and beaten to death. The only one who would speak up, who would speak the truth at the time, was the prophet Elijah. He was the only one willing to confront Ahab at the risk of his life and let the erring king know that God was not pleased by his callous wickedness.

No, Elijah was not an enemy but a friend. Sadly, because of his message he was perceived as an enemy and trouble-maker. Such will be the fate of Elijahs when they confront impenitent Ahabs.

The Bible tells us that the presentation of a truth that reproves the sins and errors of the times will excite opposition. "For everyone practicing evil hates the light and does not come to the light, lest his deeds should be exposed" (John 3:20).

Thus often, when individuals choose to cling onto their erroneous positions—in spite of the fact that those positions cannot be sustained by the Scriptures—they maliciously assail the character and motives of those who stand in defense of unpopular truth. As E. G. White perceptively observed:

> "It is the same policy which has been pursued in all ages. Elijah was declared to be a troubler in Israel, Jeremiah a traitor, Paul a polluter of the temple. From that day to this, those who would be loyal to truth have been denounced as seditious, heretical, or schismatic. Multitudes who are too unbelieving to accept the sure word of prophecy will receive with unquestioning credulity an accusation against those who dare to reprove fashionable sins. This spirit will increase more and more. And the Bible plainly teaches that a time is approaching when the laws of the state will so conflict with the law of God that whosoever would obey all the divine precepts must brave reproach and punishment as an evildoer."[31]

Shall we then conclude that the truth ought not to be presented, since it frequently arouses opposition from those who resist its claims? No! We have no more reason for holding our peace, because it excites opposition, than had Elijah, Jeremiah, Paul, and the courageous Christian Reformers.

> "The confession of faith made by saints and martyrs was recorded for the benefit of succeeding generations. Those living examples of holiness and steadfast integrity have come down to inspire courage in those who are now called to stand as witnesses for God. They received grace and truth, not for themselves alone, but that, through them, the knowledge of God might enlighten the earth. Has God given light to His servants in this generation? Then they should let it shine forth to the world."[32]

Speaking through the prophet Ezekiel, the Lord declared that "the house of Israel will not listen to you, because they will not listen to Me; for all the house of Israel are impudent and hard-hearted." Nevertheless, God said: "You shall speak My words to them, whether they hear or whether they refuse, for they are rebellious" (Ezekiel 3:7; 2:7).

Thus, whether or not we are branded "troublers of Israel" or "enemies," as opportunities extend, everyone who has received the light of truth is under the same solemn and fearful responsibility as was the prophet of Israel, to not remain silent:

> "So you, son of man: I have made you a watchman for the house of Israel; therefore you shall hear a word from My mouth and warn them for Me. When I say to the wicked, 'O wicked man, you shall surely die!' and you do not speak to warn the wicked from his way, that wicked man shall die in his iniquity; but his blood I will require at your hand. Nevertheless if you warn the wicked to turn from his way, and he does not turn from his way, he shall die in his iniquity; but you have delivered your soul." (Ezekiel 33:7–9)

The aging prophet Elijah was not deterred by the accusation of Ahab. Neither did he stoop to address the "enemy" issue. He delivered the straight and uncompromising message to Ahab. Let's listen to the dialogue:

"So Ahab said to Elijah, 'Have you found me, O my enemy?' And he answered, 'I have found you, because you have sold yourself to do evil in the sight of the Lord: "Behold, I will bring calamity on you. I will take away your posterity, and will cut off from Ahab every male in Israel, both bond and free. I will make your house like the house of Jeroboam the son of Nebat, and like the house of Baasha the son of Ahijah, because of the provocation with which you have provoked Me to anger, and made Israel sin." And concerning Jezebel the Lord also spoke, saying, "The dogs shall eat Jezebel by the wall of Jezreel. The dogs shall eat whoever belongs to Ahab and dies in the city, and the birds of the air shall eat whoever dies in the field."' But there was no one like Ahab who sold himself to do wickedness in the sight of the Lord, because Jezebel his wife stirred him up." (1 Kings 21:20–25)

We cannot but admire the courage of Elijah in confronting Ahab with the unpopular truth. It was a revolutionary act in Israel in those days, for in the words of George Orwell (1903–1950), "In an age of universal deceit, telling the truth is a revolutionary act." The prophet who had a few years earlier fled from the presence of Ahab and Jezebel regained his courage to speak up again—a voice for the voiceless.

Elijah's courage is a lesson for us all. Whatever our profession, we should always act from principle rather than policy. "We should choose the right because it is right, and leave consequences with God. To men of principle, faith, and daring, the world is indebted for its great reforms. By such men the work of reform for this time must be carried forward."[33]

Ahab's "enemy" presented the straight and uncompromising message. Elijah delivered the unpopular truth, reminding Ahab that the God who sees everything will eventually visit judgment on the murderer. The king of Israel thought no one knew of his complicity in the murder of a principled man and his innocent children. He thought he could get away with his crime. But the King of the universe had taken note and would eventually take action.

The point needs to be reiterated: When it seems as if justice has fallen in the streets—when human verdicts are bought and sold—the God of the universe still keeps a tally of such things—the God who will vindicate His own. There will be a payday someday! The certainty of this fact is affirmed several times in the Holy Scriptures:

> "Whoever digs a pit will fall into it, and he who rolls a stone will have it roll back on him." (Proverbs 26:27)

> "Those who plow iniquity and sow trouble reap the same." (Job 4:8)

> "They sow the wind, and reap the whirlwind." (Hosea 8:7)

> "Do not be deceived, God is not mocked; for whatever a man sows, that he will also reap." (Galatians 6:7, 8)

Yes, God will right all wrongs when He comes again, if not before. The great God of the universe sees all that happens on earth today, just as He saw what happened to Naboth.

THE SILENCE OF THE MAJORITY

It is impossible to study the shameful murder of Naboth and his children without the question of how these senseless deaths possibly could have happened with the concurrence of some otherwise good and respected people—the elders and nobles.

Both the Bible and the pages of history tell us that evil has often flourished because, through its silence and inaction, the majority has encouraged a few extremists to carry out their evil deeds. All one has to do to verify this fact is to look at the history of the Nazi concentration camps, the policies and practices of apartheid in South Africa, and the aggression, repression, and brutal murders by totalitarian regimes and governments—such as fascism and communism.

Even in our day, we hear the deafening silence of good people in the genocide and ethnic cleansing pogroms in many lands; in the legal killing of millions of babies at abortion facilities; and in the beheadings, hangings, firing-squads, lethal injections, and other forms of capital punishment. Even Bible-believing, born-again Christians who believe in moral absolutes are silent, because they apparently see no inconsistency in being simultaneously pro-life and pro-death penalty in their non-theocratic, democratic nations.

Again, few have the moral courage to speak out against the injustices and atrocities being committed in occupied lands by our troops and allies, including the extra-judicial targeted killings of those who resist foreign invasions or illegal occupations. We also hear the sound of deafening silence in today's state-sanctioned torture, unlawful detentions, and violations of peoples' fundamental human rights. Furthermore, because of the cowardly silence of many good people, religious and political persecutions continue to flourish in many places.

It is true that some of the senseless deaths mentioned above may not be on a par with Naboth's. This is because not all victims of indiscriminate hatred and wickedness are necessarily righteous victims of hatred against their righteousness. Yes, some of these deaths cannot be compared with the incomparably worse hatred and murder of the righteous. Still, the fact remains that the deaths of Naboth and other martyrs highlight the senselessness of all murders and the silence that often encourages them.

Why does the majority always remain silent? Why do we—elders and nobles—kill Naboths by our silence? Why is it so easy for us to be bought or sold by the Ahabs and Jezebels in power? Why are we not raising our voices against the "sons and daughters of Belial," who, with impunity, continue doing their dirty work?

Perhaps the majority of us remains silent because we simply don't care or because truth and justice are not important to us. Also, many of us remain silent because we choose to be uninformed or ignorant of the issues at stake. In some cases, we are silent because we think we are powerless to change things—either because we feel we lack the knowledge to make a stance, the skills to defend our position, or the ability or resources to effect the change. Still, some of us remain silent because we are afraid we will be persecuted in some way—we are afraid of being mocked, ostracized, attacked, deprived of our jobs, or even killed

I am sure there are other reasons why the majority is often silent. But it is worthy of note that the 1 Kings 21 account highlights another major reason why many of us are easily bought or sold. It is this: We are afraid of being labeled as "enemies" by the Ahabs and Jezebels.

UNCOMPLIMENTARY LABELS

Increasingly, many of us are selling our souls and consciences to the whims of wrong-doers, because we want to enjoy their friendship and approbation. We are not as bold as Elijah in confronting murderous Ahabs, because we are uncomfortable with their uncomplimentary labels. Few of us want to be perceived as trouble-makers. We don't want to be viewed as the enemies of the organization, institution, church, or nation.

Who wants to be perceived as "unpatriotic," or an "enemy"? Who wants to be perceived as "unpatriotic," or an "enemy"? Who wants to be branded as "controversial" or "divisive"? Who wants to face the attack or risk the ostracism of powerful political and religious leadership?

But in the grand scheme of things, in the great controversy between Truth and error, Love and hate, and Christ and Satan, *the issue is not just about choosing our friends but also about choosing our enemies.*

Inspired writings, therefore, challenge us to choose who we want to be our friends and our enemies: "Do you not know that friendship with the world is enmity with God? Whoever therefore wants to be a friend of the world makes himself an enemy of God" (James 4:4).

Those of us who don't want to be labeled as "enemies" by the Ahabs should remember that "light and darkness cannot harmonize. Between truth and error there is an irrepressible conflict. To uphold and defend the one is to attack and overthrow the other."[34]

Hence, we are admonished: "Do not be unequally yoked together with unbelievers. For what fellowship has righteousness with lawlessness? And what communion has light with darkness? And what accord has Christ with Belial? Or what part has a believer with an unbeliever?" (2 Corinthians 6:14, 15).

To be labeled by Ahabs as enemies is actually a compliment. It is an admission that we are restoring the good that Ahabs and Jezebels are destroying. We must, therefore, not be intimidated by labels. As we say in Africa, "The threatening eyes of the crocodile do not prevent the thirsty frog from drinking from the pond." In other words, fear or intimidation must never be allowed to prevent us from doing the right thing.

Those who serve God's cause must often accept the label of "enemy" or "troublemaker." They must cheerfully wear the badge of being "divisive," "controversial," or "not a team-player" in the game of Ahab and Jezebel. Such has always been the lot of all those who cannot be bought or sold.

If our preaching and teaching is an enemy to hypocrisy, then let us be enemies. If our preaching and teaching is an enemy to worldliness, then yes—we are enemies of Ahab. When people try to intimidate us, labeling us troublemakers and enemies, let us gladly accept the labels. We are in good company—with the courageous prophet Elijah!

The Scriptures call upon us to be "watchmen over Zion." If we fail to sound the alarm, the Lord holds us accountable for anyone who needlessly loses his or her life because of our negligent silence. The prophet Ezekiel warned:

"But if the watchman sees the sword coming and does not blow the trumpet to warn the people and the sword comes and takes the life of one of them, that man will be taken away because of his sin, but I will hold the watch man accountable for his blood. Son of man, I have made you a watchman for the house of Israel; so hear the word I speak and give them warning from me" Ezekiel 33:6, 7, NIV.

A silent watchman is more dangerous than no watchman, because people feel a sense of security if they know a watchman is on the job twenty-four hours a day. Therefore, we have a moral duty to speak out, take sides, and take a stand. Neutrality helps evil-doers. This is why it is a criminal act to remain silent in the face of injustice.

Uncomplimentary labels are the resort of cowardly Ahabs who are incapable of responding to the power of truth and to the unwavering commitment to principle. Their labels are calculated to exert powerful psychological pressure to coerce us into silence.

Let us refuse to be intimidated into silence when we are branded "trouble makers," "enemies," "divisive," "controversial," "extremist," "unpatriotic," or some other labels of Ahab's invention. God calls upon us—men and women—to take our stand with Naboth under the blood-stained banner of principle and integrity.

NOTES

28 E. G. White, *Patriarchs and Prophets*, p. 308.

29 Isaiah 65:6, 7; 1 Corinthians 4:5; Ecclesiastes 12:14; Matthew 12:36, 37.

30 E. G. White, *The Great Controversy*, pp. 482, 486, 487.

31 *Ibid*, pp. 458, 459.

32 *Ibid.*, p. 459.

33 *Ibid.*

34 E. G. White, *The Great Controversy*, p. 126.

PART 4
BEYON
THE ST

The Ulti

Conspir

O
ORY
nate
rcy

"I swore never to be silent whenever and wherever human beings endure suffering and humiliation. We must always take sides. Neutrality helps the oppressor, never the victim. Silence encourages the tormentor, never the tormented."

Elie Wiesel
Jewish Writer, Political Activist, Holocaust Survior and Nobel Laureate, b. 1928

ANOTHER CONSPIRACY OF SILENCE

The dictionary defines "conspiracy of silence" as an agreement among a group of people to say nothing in public about something of public interest or importance, in order to protect or promote selfish interests.

So far in our study, we've been trying to uncover the conspiracy of silence that led to the tragic death of Naboth. We have seen that his death was the result of the covetousness of a selfish king, the intrigue of an unscrupulous queen, the lies and callousness of some hired assassins, and the deafening silence of some otherwise good people.

Of the key players who were involved in Naboth's death—the Ahabs, Jezebels, sons of Belial, and the elders and nobles—we have argued that *our* role is most clearly portrayed by the "elders and nobles of Jezreel." Without the silence and inaction of this latter group, the shameful plot to murder Naboth would have come to naught.

But did you know that Naboth's trial and wrongful murder parallels that of our Lord Jesus Christ? The conspiracy of silence that attended His wrongful death was only faintly echoed in the situation of Naboth the Jezreelite.

Like Naboth, the tribunal that tried Christ was corrupt, and the accusation against Him was also blasphemy.[35] The charge against Him was made by men who were conspicuously law-breakers, and their indictment was made in the name of law, even as Jezebel had used religion and politics as cover for her action.[36] Again, false witnesses were employed to testify against Christ, the innocent One,[37] and like Naboth, He was executed outside the city gate.[38] Both Naboth and Christ were faithful unto death.[39]

As in the case of Naboth, there were many key players, so also in the case of Christ— Judas, the religious leaders, Caiaphas, Annas, Pilate, the soldiers, and the crowd. And in both instances it was the silence or inaction of some otherwise good people that ultimately led to their deaths.

In a real sense, then, Naboth's death foreshadowed that of Jesus Christ. And by studying the death of Christ, we can flesh out the specific motivations of the principal characters involved the shameful death of Naboth and all other innocent people.

WHY THE SELLOUT?

As in the case of Naboth, a number of key players participated in the plot, betrayal, and death of Jesus Christ. Observe, however, that the Bible not only identifies the many people who betrayed or "handed Christ over" to be killed but also presents to us the reasons they did so:

1. Judas: Because of greed

"Then one of the twelve, called Judas Iscariot, went to the chief priests and said, 'What are you willing to give me if I deliver Him to you?' And they counted out to him thirty pieces of silver. So from that time he sought opportunity to betray Him." (Matthew 26:14–16)

According to Matthew 26:15, it was greed or the love of money that led Judas to "deliver" Christ unto the chief priests. As a trusted disciple, Judas knew where Jesus would be found (John 18:2). After selling his Master for thirty pieces of silver—the price for a slave[40]— Judas led Christ's enemies to the Garden of Gethsemane, and while Jesus was praying with the disciples, the Bible says, Judas came and betrayed Him with a kiss—the kiss of death (Matthew 26:47–50).

2. The Religious Leaders: Because of Envy or Jealousy

"Therefore, when they [the chief priests and elders] had gathered together, Pilate said to them, 'Whom do you want me to release to you? Barabbas, or Jesus who is called Christ?' For he knew that they had handed Him over because of envy." (Matthew 27:17, 18)

"But Pilate answered them, saying, 'Do you want me to release to you the King of the Jews?' For he knew that the chief priests had handed Him over because of envy." (Mark 15:9, 10); (cf. John 12:9–11; 17–19.)

Just as Ahab's selfishness or covetousness led to the death of Naboth, so also did the spirit of envy drive the chief priests and religious leaders to drum up charges against Christ, try Him unjustly, and wrongly sentence Him to death (Matthew 26:57-68).

Envy knows no bounds. If it doesn't pout and feign ignorance, as in Ahab's case, to get what it wants, it will go any length to eliminate anyone standing in its way—as was the case of the chief priests and elders. If the chief priests had tried Jesus fairly, He would have been set free. But they did not. In fact, the trial was *illegal* and the verdict *unjust*, for several reasons:

1. Instead of a public trial, the tribunal that tried Him was secret.

2. Capital crimes were to be tried during the daytime only, but in the case of Christ, it was in the night.

3. Capital offenses were not to be tried during festival times, because it was holy time. But in the case of Christ, it was carried out during the Passover period.

4. Death penalty cases were not to be dealt with at a single sitting of one day. But Christ's trial was a speedy trial—all within twenty-four hours!

5. In trials for capital crimes, the witnesses must agree; false testimony was perjury, and the accused was to be set free. Not so, however, in Christ's case when there were conflicting testimonies from the witnesses.

Unable to come up with any credible religious charges to condemn Him to death, Caiaphas finally wanted Christ to incriminate Himself. He said: "I adjure you....Are you the Christ, the Son of God?" Jesus answered truthfully: "Thou Has Said."

And with Christ own words, the religious leaders handed Him over to Pilate. They sentenced Him to die on a religious charge of blasphemy. This charge was to appeal to the Jews, who understood that blasphemy was sin against God.

But under Roman law, blasphemy was not a charge meriting capital punishment. So when priests "handed Jesus over" to Pilate, they manufactured a new charge to appeal to the Romans—namely, sedition, or inciting a rebellion. To prove this charge, the leaders had to show that Christ was raising up a secret army for His political revolution, urging His followers not to pay taxes, or setting up a rival kingdom.

Notice that the accusation of inciting people to revolution was not true. Christ Himself had said that "he who lives by the sword shall die by the sword." Also, in His Sermon on the Mount, He had taught His follows to turn the other cheek and go the second mile. Unlike other revolutionaries who urged people not to pay taxes, Christ said, "Give to Caesar what is his, and to God what is His." And as to the claim that Jesus wanted to be a king of the Jews, a rival of Roman authority, Jesus had taught that His kingdom was not of this world.

The envy of the religious leaders led them to bribe false witnesses to say, "This fellow said, 'I am able to destroy the temple of God and build it in three days.'" This charge was designed to unite Romans and Jews, Pharisees, and Sadduccees. But even if this charge were true, it would not be reason for capital punishment. At best, it was only a boast. The truth, however, was that this charge was *not* true. What Jesus actually said was this: "Destroy this temple, and in three days I will raise it up. He spake of the temple of the His body" (John 2:21).

But observe that just as the priests were not concerned about doctrinal or moral purity, so also they were not concerned about the political stability of the nation. Their envy was driving them to lie and plot to get rid of Jesus. Thus, they had illegally tried Jesus in the night and wrongly sentenced Him, and when morning came—with the charge of political insurrection added to the charge blasphemy—the religious leaders "handed him over" to Pilate (Matt. 27:18).

So we ask again: Why did the chief priests and religious leaders do all these things? Why would they betray the Savior? The answer is: Because of *envy* or *jealousy*.[41]

3. Pilate: Because of Political Expediency

The Bible explains why Pilate also betrayed Christ—namely, he wanted to please the crowd, the religious leaders, and Caesar:

> "So Pilate, wanting to gratify the crowd, released Barabbas to them; and he delivered Jesus, after he had scourged Him, to be crucified." (Mark 15:15)

> "Then he said to them the third time, 'Why, what evil has He done?
> I have found no reason for death in Him. I will therefore chastise Him and let Him go.' But they were insistent, demanding with loud voices that He be crucified. And the voices of these men and of the chief priests prevailed. So Pilate gave sentence that it should be as they requested. And he released to them the one they requested, who for rebellion and murder had been thrown into prison; but he delivered Jesus to their will." (Luke 23:22–25)

> "From then on Pilate sought to release Him, but the Jews cried out, saying, 'If you let this Man go, you are not Caesar's friend. Whoever makes himself a king speaks against Caesar.'" (John 19:12)

Pilate's decision was one of political expediency. He didn't want to go against the nation's religious leaders, even when they were wrong. He didn't want to go against the democratic will of the people, although the people were wrong. And He didn't want to displease his boss Caesar, because he was afraid of losing his job, prestige, and position. Because he didn't want to lose his worldly power, Pilate sacrificed an innocent life.

Fear and peer pressure led Pilate to betray Jesus by compromise. Why the sellout? The answer is *political expediency*—the use of methods that bring the most immediate benefits, based on pragmatic rather than moral considerations.

4. The Crowd at the Trial: Because of Ignorance

In the end, it was the people hidden among the nameless crowd who were responsible for betraying Christ to His death. It was they who did it, for they could have stopped it when Pilate gave them the chance. But instead, they asked for the criminal Barabbas.

> "Then Pilate, when he had called together the chief priests, the rulers, and the people, said to them, 'You have brought this Man to me, as one who misleads the people. And indeed, having examined Him in your presence, I have found no fault in this Man concerning those things of which you accuse Him; no, neither did Herod, for I sent you back to him; and indeed nothing deserving of death has been done by Him. I will therefore chastise Him and release Him' (for it was necessary for him to release one to them at the feast). And they all cried out at once, saying, 'Away with this Man, and release to us Barabbas'—who had been thrown into prison for a certain rebellion made in the city, and for murder. Pilate, therefore, wishing to release Jesus, again called out to them. But they shouted, saying, 'Crucify Him, crucify Him!' Then he said to them the third time, 'Why, what evil has He done? I have found no reason for death in Him. I will therefore chastise Him and let Him go.' But they were insistent, demanding with loud voices that He be crucified. And the voices of these men and of the chief priests prevailed." (Luke 23:13–23)

Why did the anonymous people in the crowd betray Christ? The Bible explains:

> "But you denied the Holy One and the Just, and asked for a murderer to be granted to you, and killed the Prince of life, whom God raised from the dead, of which we are witnesses. And His name, through faith in His name, has made this man strong, whom you see and know. Yes, the faith which comes through Him has given him this perfect soundness in the presence of you all. Yet now, brethren, I know that you did it in igno-rance, as did also your rulers." (Acts 3:14–17, emphasis supplied; cf. 2 Corinthians 2:8)

The crowd handed Christ over to be crucified out of ignorance. Apparently, they did not fully realize what they were doing.

Significantly, the New Testament uses the same verbal form in Greek for each person or group who sold out Jesus Christ to be crucified. It is the verb *paradidomi*, meaning to "hand over" or "betray" or "deliver."

First, Judas "handed him over" to the priests (out of greed). Next, the priests "handed him over" to Pilate (out of envy). Then (out of cowardice and ambition) Pilate "handed him over" to the soldiers to be crucified—with the consent of the crowd (out of ignorance).[42]

IDENTITY OF THE ANONYMOUS

We know the names of Judas, Caiaphas, Annas, and Pilate in connection with the ultimate conspiracy to kill Christ. But the Bible does not give us the names of those in the crowd who shouted "crucify Him." Just as in the story of Naboth, where the "elders and nobles of Jezreel" are not named, so also, the nameless people hidden in the crowd at Christ's trial are not named.

Who were these individuals who betrayed or delivered (handed over) Christ?

According to the Acts 3:14-17 passage quoted above, the entire Jewish nation was responsible for Christ's death, and they did it out of ignorance. Pilate himself said to Christ: "*Your own nation* and the chief priests have delivered You to me. What have You done?" (John 18:35).

Perhaps I should mention parenthetically that the New Testament writers' assertion of the role of the nation of Israel in the death of Christ has been used wrongly through history as a justification for slandering and persecuting the Jews or for anti-semitism. However, this anti-semitic prejudice is absolutely indefensible, because the New Testament writers make absolutely clear that the Jewish people at the time of Christ were not the only people responsible for Christ's death—Herod and Pilate, Gentiles and Jews—all "conspired" against Jesus (Acts 4:27; NIV).

In fact, the Bible teaches that everyone—past and present—was involved in the conspiracy. Let's now observe how the Bible identifies those who were complicit in the betrayal and death of Christ.

On the day of Pentecost, Peter also said: "Therefore *let all the house of Israel* know assuredly that God has made this Jesus, whom *you crucified*, both Lord and Christ" (Acts 2:36). Also, Stephen, shortly before he was stoned to death also declared:

> "You stiff-necked and uncircumcised in heart and ears! You always resist the Holy Spirit; as your fathers did, so do you. Which of the prophets did your fathers not persecute? And they killed those who foretold the coming of the Just One, of whom you now have become the betrayers and murderers."
> (Acts 7:51, 52, emphasis supplied; cf. 1 Thessalonians 2:14–16)

Yes, Judas was responsible. Yes, Caiaphas and the religious leaders were responsible. Yes, Pilate was responsible. And yes, the crowd—representing the entire Jewish nation—was responsible for the criminal death of Christ. All these lighted the fuse that would burn.

However, it was not the Jewish nation alone that was hidden behind the nameless crowd. Peter and John added that *Gentiles*—that is, non-Jews—were also responsible:

"For truly against Your holy Servant Jesus, whom You anointed, both Herod and Pontius Pilate, with the Gentiles and the people of Israel, were gathered together to do whatever Your hand and Your purpose determined before to be done. Now, Lord, look on their threats, and grant to Your servants that with all boldness they may speak Your word..." (Acts 4:27, emphasis supplied)

The Gentiles refers, first, to the role of Pilate and the soldiers. For they represented the Roman superpower at that time, that could have held the Jewish nation in check. But the reference to the Gentiles goes beyond the Roman power in the first century. *The Gentiles also include all people—both then and now.*

The Gentiles hidden behind the faceless crowd at the trial and crucifixion of Christ *includes us!* For the Bible tells us that any time we sin, we "crucify...the Son of God afresh, and put him to an open shame" (Hebrews 6:6)!

So we come in full circle as the culprits at Naboth's trial—the "elders and nobles." Those whose silence and inaction led to the shameful death of Naboth, are the same people hidden behind the nameless crowd at Christ's trial and death. *And we are the ones!*

It's a fact that Judas handed Christ over to the religious leaders—because of money (greed). It's true that the religious leaders handed Him over to Pilate—because of envy/jealousy. It's also a fact that Pilate handed Him over to the soldiers—because of fear/ambition. And it's true that the Roman soldiers were responsible for nailing Christ to the cross—because they were following orders. But the critical link in this chain of responsibility is the nameless people who shouted "crucify Him."

The crowd—representing all of us—could have stayed the wrongful death of Christ if it had chosen to do so. But it did not. Its silence and inaction were ultimately responsible. The Roman soldiers, Pilate, chief priests and elders, and Judas could only succeed in murdering Christ because the nameless crowd allowed it.

"Most of the evils of this world have come into being, not by the direct intention of any one in particular, but in every case through the co-operation of all of us giving them a push by some word or by some silence, for which we are responsible; and though at the time it may have seemed a small thing, the word we spoke, or the word we failed to speak, yet in so far as our act could have restrained or diverted or qualified the order of events, we are as responsible for it as though we had with our own hand done the deed."[43]

So, just as Naboth's death pointed to Christ's own, the key players in Christ's death shed further light on the motivations of all those involved in the death of faithful Naboths. All of us are guilty of betraying and murdering Christ. Like the nameless people, we sing "Hosanna," spread our clothes on the floor for Him to walk on, and then cry out, "crucify Him!" We are the elders and nobles of Jezreel.

The old Negro Spiritual asks the question, "Were you there when they crucified my Lord?" The answer is, "Yes, we were there"! We were there alongside Judas, Herod, Pilate, Gentiles, and Jews. The noted British Evangelical scholar and preacher, John Stott, sums it up thus:

> "If we were in their place, we would have done what they did. Indeed, we *have* done it. For whenever we turn away from Christ, we 'are crucifying the Son of God all over again and subjecting him to public disgrace' (Heb. 6:6). We too sacrifice Jesus to our greed like Judas, to our envy like the priests, to our ambition like Pilate.... 'Yes, we were there.' Not as spectators only but as participants, guilty participants, plotting, scheming, betraying, bargaining, and handing him over to be crucified. We may try to wash our hand of responsibility like Pilate. But our attempt will be as futile as his. For there is blood on our hands. Before we can begin to see the cross as something done *for* us (leading us to faith and worship), we have to see it as something done *by* us (leading us to repentance)."[44]

We must take ownership of our silence and inactions and ask the Lord for forgiveness. We must then resolve, by the grace of God, that never again under our watch will we be a party to injustice. The Bible tells us that during the time of ignorance, God overlooks, but now commands all men to repent (Acts 17:31).

When we acknowledge our wrong-doing and turn from our ways, there is forgiveness for us. There is hope for all the elders and nobles—all the nameless in the crowd—if only they will repent.

PARDON FOR THE UNPARDONABLE

Can God pardon those whose cowardly silence has led to the death of the innocent? Is there hope for people who have knowingly and even ignorantly committed the most awful sins?

Yes, indeed, God *can* and *will* forgive. Christ's dying prayer on Calvary's cross is the greatest evidence that forgiveness is available to all. His prayer, "Father, forgive them, for they don't know what they are doing" (Luke 23:32), is proof that not only will God forgive the actions of all those involved in the death of Christ—but also every sinner who is willing to accept His offer of forgiveness.

Christ uttered those dying words when He was being crucified—a repugnant, demeaning form of execution for the rabble and miscreants of society. When the Bible says Jesus "humbled Himself, and became obedient unto death, *even the death of the cross*" (Philippians 2:8), the italicized phrase is referring to the shameful method of death that was reserved for the worst offenders.

Though the New Testament itself doesn't go into details, contemporary documents of those times tell us what crucifixion was like:

> "The prisoner would first be publicly humiliated by being stripped naked. He was then laid on his back on the ground, while his hands were either nailed or roped to the horizontal wooden beam (the *patibulum*), and his feet to the vertical pole. The cross was then hoisted to an upright position and dropped into a socket which had been dug for it in the ground. Usually a peg or rudimentary seat was provided to take some of the weight of the victim's body and prevent it from being torn loose. But there he would hang, helplessly exposed to intense physical pain, public ridicule, daytime heat and night-time cold. The torture would last several days."[45]

Anyone crucified was viewed with utmost contempt. In fact, it was almost an obscenity to discuss crucifixion in polite society. The Roman lawyer and philosopher Cicero (103 B.C.–43 B.C.) wrote: "This very word 'cross' should be removed not only from the person of a Roman citizen but from his thoughts, his eyes, his ears." The Roman authorities reserved the cross for rebellious slaves and conquered people and for notorious robbers and assassins.

Death by crucifixion was designed to exert maximum pain. Because of the torture involved in such deaths, a dying man might scream, curse, or utter threats. Rarely would a word of forgiveness be heard from a person being crucified. Jesus, however, responded in a very unusual way to His own crucifixion. The Bible records the event at Calvary this way:

"There were also two others, criminals, led with Him to be put to death. And when they had come to the place called Calvary, there they crucified Him, and the criminals, one on the right hand and the other on the left. Then Jesus said, 'Father, forgive them, for they do not know what they do.' And they divided His garments and cast lots. And the people stood looking on. But even the rulers with them sneered, saying, 'He saved others; let Him save Himself if He is the Christ, the chosen of God.' The soldiers also mocked Him, coming and offering Him sour wine, and saying, 'If You are the King of the Jews, save Yourself.' And an inscription also was written over Him in letters of Greek, Latin, and Hebrew: THIS IS THE KING OF THE JEWS." (Luke 23:32–38)

On Calvary's cross, Jesus didn't offer a word in His own defense. He didn't condemn those responsible for His death. He didn't proclaim His own innocence. He did not allow His suffering of injustice to turn Him against God. He didn't utter any curses or attack His attackers. He didn't attempt to save Himself. And He did not blame anyone—though many were to blame. Instead, He said, "*Father forgive them, for they know not what they do*" (Luke 23:34)!

No one standing near the cross expected Christ to offer forgiveness to those who were hurting Him. Yet He did. The amazing thing at Calvary was that while our Lord Jesus was being crucified, He "kept praying" for His murderers that God would forgive them! The only words that kept coming from His lips were words of forgiveness, even explaining the reason for the action of His murderers: "For they do not know what they are doing"!

It is simply amazing: Calvary, the place where human beings did their worst, was also where God did His best. On the cross, God displayed His love for those who showed their hatred and contempt. Calvary is the place where Christ stretched out His arms, beckoning all humanity to come unto Him. For in His most agonizing moment, Christ prays for His killers: "Father, forgive them, for they don't know what they are doing."

Christ's offer of forgiveness to those murdering Him was an incredible act. But the act also raises two profound questions: 1) Why forgive a person for what he does not know he is doing? And 2) Who are the "they" for whom Christ prayed?

1. The Guilt of Ignorance
The first question arising from Christ's dying prayer—namely, "Why forgive a person for what he does not know he is doing?"—raises the issue of the "guilt of ignorance." Can a person be held accountable for an offence of which he or she is not aware?

Notice that Jesus did not say that all sins done in ignorance lose, on that ground, their sinful character. Although the people "did not know what they were doing," yet they needed forgiveness, and Christ offered it. This fact reveals that ignorance does not absolve one of moral blame. Forgiveness is only needed for the guilty. Nobody can forgive an innocent person. So when Jesus said, "Father, forgive them," He meant they were guilty. Then when He said, "For they don't know what they are doing," at the very least He meant, "they should have known what they were doing. And they are guilty for not knowing what they are doing." That is why they needed to be forgiven.

In other words, "I did not know" is not an excuse to absolve us from wrong-doing. Ignorance and guilt are not mutually exclusive. A person may do wrong ignorantly, yet be blameworthy, and therefore need forgiveness.

The Bible, therefore, teaches such a thing as "sinning through ignorance." Though this particular sin may differ in degree from willful, premeditated sin (and hence punishment or moral responsibility may differ on that account), it is sin, nonetheless.[46] Our Lord Himself confirms this teaching of "sinning through ignorance" when He taught that "he who did not know, yet committed things deserving of stripes, shall be beaten with few" (Luke 12:48).

But it should also be observed that Christ's prayer on the cross not only declares our guilt—even the guilt resulting from our sins of ignorance—but also offers forgiveness at the same time. His prayer declares that we are guilty, *and* He simultaneously offers forgiveness. Not only did He say, "for they don't know what they are doing," but He also says, "Father, forgive them."

2. Extent of God's Forgiveness

The second question raised by Christ prayer at Calvary is this: Who was He talking about when He said, "For *they* know not what they are doing?" Who are the "they" He was talking about, and who are the "them" for whom He was requesting forgiveness? This question has to do with the extent of God's forgiveness.

The immediate context of Christ's prayer suggests that He was referring to the *Roman soldiers*. They were the ones carrying out the execution. They were the ones who were doing the dirty deed. They were the ones nailing Him to the cross. No doubt they had watched the proceedings of the trial and had seen Christ's demeanor all through the process. Like one of the soldiers at the cross who "glorified God, saying, 'Certainly this was a righteous Man!'" (Luke 23:47), the soldiers who nailed Christ to the cross could have known that He was innocent. Yet, they killed Him, perhaps on the lame excuse that they were just following orders. They were guilty.

But, the "they" in Christ's prayer also included the whole *Roman government, with Pontius Pilate* as its representative. Pilate could have changed the outcome. He could have followed his own gut conviction, if not the Roman law. He didn't have to cave in to the pressure of the crowd and the lure of his own ambition. He could have done something, but he didn't. Even when his own wife, warned in a dream, urged him to set Christ free, he didn't. He was guilty.

Included in the "they" are also the *religious authorities and the crowd at the trial.* They were the ones who, preferring Barabbas over Christ, handed Jesus over to Pilate. They knew, or should have known (like Nicodemus, the ruler of the synagogue) that Jesus was the Messiah. But when given the opportunity by Pilate to set Jesus free, they cried out, "Crucify Him!" They also were guilty.

And yes, the "they" also included *Judas*—the disciple who sold Jesus to the religious rulers. He was privy to Christ's teachings and had been the object of Christ's personal entreaties.[47] Yet he joined in the plot to kill his Master.

But there is more to the "they." When Christ asked His Father for forgiveness, saying, "they don't know what they are doing," the "they" also included Christ's *own followers—the disciples who abandoned Him in the hour of His greatest need.* They probably could not have changed the course of events in opposition to the Roman army, the government authority, and the religious leaders. But they could have done something. They could have stood by Him, stayed with Him, been loyal to Him, and showed Him they cared. But they were afraid. They hid themselves away. They closed themselves in, cowering behind locked doors.

Above all, the "they" is a reference to *all of us*. As we have shown in the previous section, both *Jews and Gentiles* are complicit in the shameful death of Christ. This includes *you and me*—those of us who daily crucify Christ afresh by our sins. Like all the others, we also are guilty, even if we are ignorant. For we should have known better—at least we could have known.

Yes, we can identify some of the guilty ones by name: Judas, Annas, Caiaphas, Herod, Pilate, and Peter. In addition, the Roman soldiers were also guilty, and so were the other Jewish leaders—the Pharisees and the scribes who conspired to put Him to death. The unnamed individuals in the crowd at the trial were also guilty. The spectators who were at Calvary to cheer, laugh, and mock were guilty. The entire nation of Israel and all Gentiles were guilty. And yes, we also are guilty. We are included among the "they."

Although guilty, Christ prayed for us all, saying, "Father, forgive them, for *they* don't know what they are doing."

The significance of Christ's dying prayer at Calvary is made more explicit in a prophecy recorded in Isaiah 53. In this Messianic prophecy, the prophet Isaiah explains that Christ's prayer was not just for them—the people who were immediately responsible for His death—but for all of us: "Because He poured out His soul unto death, and He was numbered with the transgressors, and *He bore the sin of many, and made intercession for the transgressors*" (Isaiah 53:12).

At Calvary Christ "bore the sin of many, and made intercession for the transgressors." When the Bible says Christ bore the sins of "many," it means *all* sinners who accept His offer of salvation by believing in Him.[48] He made "intercession" for all sinners—that is, He prayed for all of us. This is the glory of the Christian gospel.

3. The Glory of the Gospel

Christ's prayer at the cross is the heart and glory of the Christian gospel—namely, that forgiveness is available to all who are willing to accept it. On Calvary's cross full atonement was made for the guilt of all sinners—covetous, envious, proud, liars, drunkards, prostitutes, adulterers, sexually immoral, racists, robbers, rebellious, murderers, etc. There is mercy for all who are willing to accept it.

In anticipation of this marvelous event at Calvary, the Old Testament prophets declared, "'Come now, let us reason together,' says the Lord. 'Though your sins are like scarlet, they shall be as white as snow; though they are red as crimson, they shall be like wool'" (Isaiah 1:18). Scarlet sins will be made as white as snow!

In a sense, the Bible can be read as a record of how God forgave sinners and transformed them into saints. For example, there was forgiveness for

- King David's sins of adultery, dishonesty, and murder.

- The many sins of the woman of Luke 7.

- The prodigal son's riotous living in a distant city.

- Simon Peter's triple denial of Christ by swearing and profanity.

- Zacchaeus, a public robber.

- Mary Magdalene, a common harlot.

- Saul of Tarsus's merciless persecution of Christians.

- The Corinthian church member who slept with his father's wife.

Though sin is offensive to God, and though unconfessed sin can cost us our salvation, if we acknowledge our wrong-doing and change our ways, God will forgive us. The experience of the believers in the church of Corinth can be ours too:

> "Do you not know that the unrighteous will not inherit the kingdom of God? Do not be deceived. Neither fornicators, nor idolaters, nor adulterers, nor homosexuals, nor sodomites, nor thieves, nor covetous, nor drunkards, nor revilers, nor extortioners will inherit the kingdom of God. And such were some of you. *But you were washed, but you were sanctified, but you were justified in the name of the Lord Jesus and by the Spirit of our God.*" (1 Corinthians 6:9–11, emphasis supplied)[49]

God's forgiveness knows no bounds. Writes the Psalmist: "If You, Lord, should mark iniquities, O Lord, who could stand? But there is forgiveness with You, that You may be feared" (Psalm 130:3, 4).

Do we need further evidence of God's willingness to forgive? Look at King Ahab. After all that he did—after selling himself to do wickedly, even after his role in Naboth's death—when he outwardly expressed his remorse for his sins, God was willing to show him mercy. After hearing the message of judgment from Elijah the prophet on the apostate king, he apparently humbled himself before God:

"But there was no one like Ahab who sold himself to do wickedness in the sight of the Lord, because Jezebel his wife stirred him up. And he behaved very abominably in following idols....So it was, when Ahab heard those words [from Elijah], that he tore his clothes and put sackcloth on his body, and fasted and lay in sackcloth, and went about mourning. And the word of the Lord came to Elijah the Tishbite, saying, 'See how Ahab has humbled himself before Me? Because he has humbled himself before Me, I will not bring the calamity in his days. In the days of his son I will bring the calamity on his house.'" (1 Kings 21:25–29)

Indications from the Bible are that Ahab's "repentance" was not genuine.[50] Even if Ahab was not truly repentant, God's temporary delay of His judgment upon the king of Israel offers hope to all who truly repent: If God was willing to spare for a while someone who had, at best, only partially repented, what will He do for the one who sincerely repents? In the words of Matthew Henry, "If a pretending partial penitent shall go to his house reprieved, doubtless a sincere penitent shall go to his house justified."[51]

Although God will punish unrepentant evil-doers, the Bible makes clear that He is "merciful and gracious, longsuffering, and abounding in goodness and truth, keeping mercy for thousands, forgiving *iniquity and transgression and sin.*"[52]

Each of these three words has a different connotation. *Iniquity* has to do with moral evil. *Transgression* signifies revolt or rebellion. Sin means an offence against the Most High God. These three terms cover every kind of evil possible. Whatever category of sin, God forgives it all.

The theme of divine forgiveness is at the very heart of the good news about Jesus Christ. When we acknowledge our sins, confess them, and make a commitment to turn away from them, Christ is always ever anxious to forgive us. The Psalmist says: "For You, Lord, are good, and ready to forgive, and abundant in mercy to all those who call upon You" (Psalm 86:5).

Christ's dying prayer at Calvary assures us that the Lord will never cast away a truly repentant soul. The following promises of His willingness to forgive will dispel any lingering doubts:

> "'Come now, and let us reason together,' says the Lord, 'Though your sins are like scarlet, they shall be as white as snow; though they are red like crimson, they shall be as wool.'" (Isaiah 1:18)

> "For You have cast all my sins behind Your back." (Isaiah 38:17)

> "As far as the east is from the west, so far has He removed our transgressions from us." (Psalm 103:12)

> "Who is a God like You, pardoning iniquity and passing over the transgression of the remnant of His heritage? He does not retain His anger forever, because He delights in mercy." (Micah 7:18)

> "Let the wicked forsake his way, and the unrighteous man his thoughts; let him return to the Lord, and He will have mercy on him; and to our God, for He will abundantly pardon." (Isaiah 55:7)

That God will forgive is further evidenced by the fact that among the 3,000 who repented and were baptized on the day of Pentecost were some of the people who had earlier on shouted, "Crucify Him" (Acts 2:36-41).

No sin is so dark that God won't forgive. We cannot out-sin the forgiveness of God *if* we truly repent, confess, and ask for forgiveness: "If we confess our sins, He is faithful and just to forgive us our sins and to cleanse us from all unrighteousness" (1 John 1:9).

As "elders and nobles of Jezreel," our silence and inaction caused the death of principled Naboth and sinless Christ. However, if we repent—if we turn from our wrong-doing—God will *forgive* us and *cleanse* us from *all* unrighteousness. The message from Calvary's cross is that forgiveness is freely available to all who believe.

There's only one situation in which finding forgiveness is difficult. If we choose to remain in denial, if we remain unrepentant, Heaven cannot forgive us for our complicity in the betrayal and murder of the innocent ones. That is, if we don't desire forgiveness, if we don't ask for it, or if we persistently refuse to respond to the invitation to repent, it is impossible to receive His forgiveness.

We bear full responsibility for our silence and inaction in the shameful injustices that the innocent suffer. And the truth demands a response. For when confronted with the truth, an honestly mistaken person either ceases to be mistaken or ceases to be honest.

When we acknowledge and repent of our sin, the Lord will not only forgive us, He will totally cleanse us of all our wrong-doing. In gratitude, we resolve that never again under our watch will we be silent. And enabled by His grace, we begin to live a life that is true to principle.

NOTES

35 Matthew 26:59, 65.

36 Matthew 26:59, 60; John 19:7; cf. John 18:31.

37 Mark 14:55-61.

38 Hebrews 13:12; cf. John 19:16-20.

39 Philippians 2:8.

40 Exodus 21:32; cf. Zechariah 11:12.

41 Observe that, although the words *envy* and *jealousy* are often used interchangeably, there is a subtle difference between the two terms. It is said that, "Envy is angry at what everyone else has that it does not possess. Jealousy is afraid that what it owns will be taken away by someone else. Envy begins with empty hands, mourning its lack but joying when others lose their superiority. Jealousy begins with full hands, fearful of losing what it has already achieved to someone else" Karl A. Olsson, *Seven Sins and Seven Virtues*, (New York: Harper & Brothers, 1962), 24. In either case, whoever cherishes jealousy or envy is not content with what he/she has or is.

42 Matthew 26:14-16 (Judas); 27:18 (the priests); 27:26 (Pilate); Acts 7:52 (the verbal form used is *prodidōmi*).

43 *Speaker's Bible*, Luke, p. 156.

44 John W. Stott, *The Cross of Christ* (Downers Grove, IL: InterVarsity, 1986), pp. 59, 60.

45 Stott, *The Cross of Christ*, p. 48. A summary of available information about crucifixion can be found in Martin Hengel's *Crucifixion*, translated by John Bowden (Minneapolis, MN: Fortress Press, 1977).

46 This fact is also plainly taught in the Old Testament: "If a person sins, and commits any of these things which are forbidden to be done by the commandments of the Lord, though he does not know it, yet he is guilty and shall bear his iniquity. And he shall bring to the priest a ram without blemish from the flock, with your valuation, as a trespass offering. So the priest shall make atonement for him regarding his igno-rance in which he erred and did not know it, and it shall be forgiven him" (Leviticus 5:17, 18). Thus, sins done in ignorance are still sin. Those who commit such sins need forgiveness, just as much as those who commit willful sins. In the New Testament we read that during the "times of ignorance God overlooked, but now commands all men everywhere to repent" (Acts 17:30). If one has to repent for things done in ignorance, the implication is that those acts are sin. Though one's punishment may be mitigated by certain factors, ignorance does not absolve one from the punishment one deserves. The apostle Paul judges his own past life on the same principle of "sinning through ignorance." When he persecuted the church, he did it ignorantly. He was honestly mistaken. He was "the least of the apostles," not worthy to be called an apostle because he persecuted the Church of God" (1 Corinthians 15:9).

47 See, for example, Matthew 26:17-25; John 12:1-7; 13:18-30.

48 That the "many" is a reference to all who believe is evident in a number of Bible passages. For example, referring to Christ's statement that He came in order to give "His life a *ransom* for many" (Matthew 20:28; Mark 10:45), the apostle Paul explains: "For there is one God, and one mediator between God and men, the man Christ Jesus; Who gave himself a *ransom for all*, to be testified in due time" (1 Timothy 2:5, 6). In other words, the "many" is not restrictive to a few people, but is to all—that is, to all who believe: "But *as many as received him*, to them gave he power to become the sons of God, even to them that believe on his name" (John 1:12). And in the favorite Bible passage, "For God so loved the world that He gave His only begotten Son, that *whoever believes in Him* should not perish but have everlasting life" (John 3:16).

49 The use of the past tense in 1 Corinthians 6:11 emphasizes that what the Corinthians were in the past is not what they are in the present, because they have been changed. The process by which this change takes place is defined by three terms: cleansing, sanctification, and justification. In the Greek, each verb is introduced by the strong adversative conjunction *alla*, a word normally translated in English as "but." Thus, the KJV states: "*but* ye are washed, *but* ye are sanctified, *but* ye are justified. . . ." The force of the word "but" (*alla*) is that it expresses a sharp contrast to what has come before. It also has a confirming or emphatic nuance. In other words, there was a radical difference between what the Corinthians were in the past and what they currently became when they were converted. The completeness of the forgiveness and transformation of the Corinthians can be ours today, when we acknowledge our wrong-doing and confess our sins.

50 Although Ahab's demonstration of repentance was striking and impressive, there are indications in the Bible that his repentance was not genuine. For example, there is no record that he did anything to repudiate or reduce the evil influence of Jezebel in the kingdom. He apparently still clung to the worship of Jezebel's imported idols. Thus, when on one occasion he and Jehoshaphat, king of Judah, decided to go to war against the Syrians, Ahab consulted with four hundred false prophets (1 Kings 22:6). If Ahab had been truly repentant, he would have cut himself loose from these false prophets. More telling is Ahab's reaction to the request by righteous king Jehoshaphat for a second opinion after the four hundred false prophets assured Ahab of success in the battle against Syria. To Jehoshaphat's question, "*Is there* not still a prophet of the Lord here, that we may inquire of Him?" Ahab replied: "*There* is still one man, Micaiah the son of Imlah, by whom we may inquire of the Lord; but I hate him, because he does not prophesy good concerning me, but evil" (1 Kings 22:7, 8). The fact that this prophet, Micaiah, had nothing good to say about Ahab indicates that the king of Israel had not truly repented of his sin, and Ahab's confession of his hatred for a servant of God ought to remove all question about his spiritual condition. In the light of the forgoing, we can only conclude that Ahab's act in tearing his clothes, putting on sackcloth, fasting, and mourning after hearing the message of judgment from Elijah was not genuine. He was motivated by the fear of judgment to come than the magnitude of his sins. In this respect, Ahab's "repentance" is no different from other false conversions recorded in the Bible: Esau (Heb. 12:16, 17); Judas Iscariot (Acts 1:16-20); Simon Magus (Acts 8:9-24); and Demas (2 Tim. 4:10).

51 Matthew Henry, *Commentary on the Whole Bible*, 7 volumes. Volume II (Joshua to Esther) (Hendrickson Publishers, 1991), 2:699.

52 Exodus 34:6, 7; emphasis supplied.

PART 5
UNFOL
STORY

Being T
to Princ

DING

ue

ple

"Silence is more eloquent than words."

Thomas Carlyle
Scottish Historian and Essayist,
1795–1881

TOTAL SURRENDER OF SELF

As explained in the Introduction to this book, the initial impetus for this work was the assignment to speak on the first quality described in the now-familiar insightful statement:

> "The greatest want of the world is the want of men—*men who will not be bought or sold*, men who in their inmost souls are true and honest, men who do not fear to call sin by its right name, men whose conscience is as true to duty as the needle to the pole, men who will stand for the right though the heavens fall" (*Education*, p. 57).

To explore what it means to be "men who will not be bought or sold," we decided to investigate the passage in 1 Kings 21 and draw applications for today. In the course of our study, we looked at Naboth, a man of honor who stood by his convictions without wavering. In contrast, the passage also presents to us Ahab and other key players who allowed themselves to be bought and who put selfish interests before morality—a fact that led them to murder an innocent individual.

But the above "greatest want of the world" statement, which sparked this investigation, did not just stop at "men who will stand for the right though the heavens fall." It continues with two equally important sentences:

> "But such a character is not the result of accident; it is not due to special favors or endowments of Providence. *A noble character is the result of self-discipline*, of the subjection of the lower to the higher nature—*the surrender of self for the service of love to God and man.*"

Being true to principle doesn't just happen. Since selfishness or self-interest lies at the root of our cowardly silence and inaction, taking ownership of our complicity in injustices calls for a dying to self. The "surrender of self for the service of love to God and man" is the beginning of an uncompromising life of integrity.

This fact is remarkably illustrated in the definite reason Naboth gave for refusing to sell his vineyard to Ahab: "*The Lord forbid it, that I should give the inheritance of my fathers unto thee.*" (1 Kings 21:3).

Observe that the simple reason why the vineyard was not for sale was his loyalty to "the Lord" and his fidelity to the "inheritance of my fathers." Naboth totally surrendered his personal self-interest "for the service of love to God and man."

In his "service of love *to God*," Naboth correctly understood that selling the vineyard would be to disrespect God as the ultimate owner of all land. Such an action would have betrayed the trust reposed in him as a faithful steward of God. True love for God is displayed in obeying Him. This is why Jesus said, "*If you love me, keep my commandments*" (John 14:15).

Also in his "service of love *to...man*," Naboth clearly understood that the land was given not just to him but to his entire family—not just his immediate relatives but his whole family that had gone centuries before him and his family that would come generations after him. He couldn't betray this obligation, either. If loving God with all our hearts "is the first and great commandment," according to Jesus, "the second is like it: '*You shall love your neighbor as yourself.*' On these two commandments hang all the Law and the Prophets." (Matthew 22:38-40).

Thus, from Naboth's example, we learn that to surrender one's self is to put the interests of God and other human beings ahead of one's own. This is the first step toward a life of integrity. In contrast, Ahab, Jezebel, the sons of Belial, and the elders and nobles did not fully understand, appreciate, or possess this spirit of total surrender of self.

Ironically, the most insightful definition of total surrender in the Scriptures comes from the lips of Ahab, the covetous king of Israel, when he surrendered to King Benhadad of Syria. "And the king of Israel...said, *My lord, O King, according to your saying I am yours and all that I have.*" (1 Kings 20:4, NKJV).

When I willingly surrender to the Lord Jesus Christ, I am in effect saying to Him, "My Lord, O King, according to Your saying, I am Yours and all that I have." Notice the following essential elements when I surrender to Christ:

1. Jesus becomes my "Lord and King"—I become His servant.

2. Christ's Word becomes supreme in my life. Whether it seems reasonable or unreasonable, I am willing to order my life "according to His saying." I do not independently hold on to my own opinions or ideas—my life is directed by what He says in His Word.

3. My very being or self belongs to Jesus. When I tell Him, "I *am* Yours," that includes my thoughts, my will, my affections, my desires, my relationships, my rights, etc.—they all belong to Him.

4. "All that I *have*" also belongs to Jesus. The "all" includes everything I claim as my own—my time, wealth, abilities, accomplishments, reputation, etc.—they all belong to my Lord Jesus Christ.

The beginning of an uncompromising life of integrity is a surrender of self to the service of God and to our fellow men. But there is more. Being true to principle also calls for a clear understanding of things that cannot be bought or sold.

KNOWING WHAT IS NOT FOR SALE

It is said that "every man has his price." That is, there is something for which everyone will be found willing to sell himself. We may be bought with one temptation or another—honors, profits, or pleasures of one class or another. For these, some would sell their conscience, the salvation their souls, the favor of God, etc.

Not so, however, with Naboth. His reply to Ahab's request for his vineyard shows that certain things simply are not for sale. We must not part with them through the force of temptation or the threat of persecution or death. To sell those things is to sell our identity, ancestral inheritance, and spiritual integrity and loyalty. We must faithfully guard those things at any cost.

When Naboth said to Ahab, "*The Lord forbid it me*, that I should give the inheritance of my fathers unto thee" (1 Kings 21:3), his reply reveals that he was a conscientious man—a true believer. His actions arose from a clear understanding of what he believed and a sterling conviction about his duty to God as the Supreme Lawgiver. Hence, he would rather offend a human being than violate God's will. He would rather incur the wrath of a vengeful Ahab and Jezebel than to displease God.

The reply of Naboth is similar to the answer of the New Testament apostles, when forbidden to preach in Jesus' name. The apostles recognized that divine obligations take priority over human legislation. And because they would "obey God rather than man" (Acts 5:29), they were ready to undergo persecution, torture, or death rather than disobey God. They would rather die than sin.

Through the years men and women have often sold themselves, their inheritance, and consciences for some temporary gain or pleasure. Such men and women stand in stark contrast to the faithful:

- Esau sold his inheritance for *food*. Not so with Naboth, who refused to sell his inheritance, regardless of the price Ahab was willing to pay. Similarly, when the king of Babylon offered the four Hebrew boys food that would have defiled them, they refused to compromise their faith (Daniel 1:8).

- Samson sold his ministry and career for *lust*. Not so with Joseph, the son of Jacob. He would not sell his integrity by yielding to Mrs. Potiphar's sexual advances.

- Gehazi sold his ministry for *riches*. Not so with his master Elisha, who refused the riches from Naaman (2 Kings 5). And not so with Daniel, who refused to accept money for the interpretation of the dream for King Belshazzar (Daniel 5:17).

- Herod sold John the Baptist's head to Herodias because of the *applause* of "those who sat." Not so with Vashti, who refused to display her beauty publicly for the applause of her husband, the king, and his men (Esther 1). And not so with Shadrach, Meshach, and Abednego, who were willing to be burned in the fiery furnace rather than receive the applause of King Nebuchadnezzar.

- Pilate sold his conscience for *power*. Not so with Moses, who was willing to give up the power of being the next pharoah, choosing instead to suffer with God's people (Hebrews 11:24, 25).

The above examples highlight the need for us to be clear about the things in life that cannot be bought or sold. Often, they are things that have been bequeathed unto us at a great price. And we sell them at a terrible price. Some of these things are:

1. **A Good Name:** "A *good name* is to be chosen rather than great riches, loving favor rather than silver and gold" (Proverbs 22:1; cf. Ecclesiastes 7:1).

   A "good name" is a reference to our character. Wealth, impressive academic degrees, accomplishments, and position can earn us good reputation, but they cannot offer good character. Character is what we really are, while reputation is merely what others think we are. Character cannot be bought or sold.

2. **Cherished Inheritance:** "See that no one is…godless like Esau, who for a single meal sold his *inheritance rights* as the oldest son" (Hebrews 12:16).

   Inheritance rights refers to those things that have been passed from generation to generation and which embody future hopes and expectations. They are often captured in historical icons, such as the constitutions of nations—or the distinctive belief systems of churches and religions. These "faith of our fathers" legacies are also not for sale. To lose them is to lose our sense of history and direction

3. **Soul's salvation:** "For what is a man profited, if he shall gain the whole world, and lose his own soul? Or *what shall a man give in exchange for his soul?*" (Matthew 16:26).

   Nothing is so precious in life as the salvation of our souls—as gaining eternal life. Unfortunately, we often allow work, busy-ness, and the pursuit of human relationships and the allurements of this world to hinder us from securing our greatest need—the grace of God.

4. **A Saving Knowledge of Christ:** "You were not redeemed with corruptible things, like silver or gold, from your aimless conduct received by tradition from your fathers, but with the precious blood of Christ, as of a lamb without blemish and without spot" (1 Peter 1:18, 19).

Salvation from a life of sin cannot be bought or sold. It is a gift from God, made possible through Jesus Christ, who died for our sin: "For God so loved the world that He gave His only begotten Son, that whoever believes in Him should not perish but have everlasting life" (John 3:16). We obtain this gift by knowing Jesus as our Savior and Lord: "And this is eternal life, that they may know You, the only true God, and Jesus Christ whom You have sent" (John 17:3; cf. 1 John 5:13).

5. **The Gift of Holy Spirit:** "Your money perish with you, because you thought that the gift of God [the Holy Spirit] could be purchased with money!" (Acts 8:20) The Holy Spirit is freely given as a guarantee, a down payment or "pledge of our inheritance."[53]

Without the Holy Spirit we shall have dead consciences. The Holy Spirit reveals truth to us, convicts us of sin, prompts us to right-doing, and empowers us for service (John 16:7-15; 1 Corinthians 12). The Spirit cannot be obtained by money or through gimmicks invented by human beings. We receive the gift of the Holy Spirit by repentance and a loving obedience to God:

"Repent, and let every one of you be baptized in the name of Jesus Christ for the remission of sins; and you shall receive the gift of the Holy Spirit....And we are His [Christ's] witnesses to these things, and so also is the Holy Spirit whom God has given to those who obey Him" (Acts 2:38; 5:32). "If you love Me, keep My commandments. And I will pray the Father, and He will give you another Helper, that He may abide with you forever—the Spirit of truth..." (John 14:15–17)

Only when so received can we have a clean conscience. Unfortunately, Governor Felix thought he could purchase a clean conscience with money (Acts 24:24–26). But this work of the Spirit on human hearts is also not for sale

6. **The Word of God.** Infinitely more precious than anything this world has to offer is the Word of God. Writing about the value of the Holy Scriptures, David says: "More to be desired are they than gold, yea, than much fine gold; sweeter also than honey and the honeycomb" (Psalm 19:10).

In both Psalm 119 and Psalm 19:7–19 David describes the multifaceted purpose of Scripture, when he describes it as "the law of the Lord," "the testimony of the Lord," "the precepts of the Lord," the "commandment of the Lord," "the fear of the Lord," and "the judgments of the Lord." Because of the immense value of the Word of God, we cannot exchange it for any other human authority. It is the sole and authoritative norm for belief and practice. (2 Timothy 3:16, 17; Isaiah 8:19, 20)

We must be clear in our minds about those things in life that cannot be bought or sold. As we pointed out earlier, Naboth would have gladly obliged the request of Ahab which seemed so reasonable and appealing. And if he had complied and sold his vineyard, he would have been honored and rewarded by the king. But he understood clearly that at stake were his identity, his ancestral heritage, and his spiritual integrity. These things were not for sale.

Hence, Naboth was willing to stand by his convictions—and was faithful even to the very end.

In these critical times, we face strong temptations to compromise the inheritance of our fathers. As in the days of Naboth, so also in our day.

- Ahab wants us to trade in the faith of our fathers for his "vegetable garden"—his new designer gospels, custom-made to suit his covetous spirit.

- He wants to merge our vineyard to his, because it is "near his house"—he wants to swallow our distinctive faith in his false ecumenical alliances.

- Ahab wants us to "exchange" our Christian lifestyle practices, music, and worship style for his watered-down version.

- He even promises to "pay" us for it with promises of explosive numerical church growth—often at the expense of sound biblical teaching and authentic biblical spirituality.

When the lure of compromise and seemingly harmless violations whispers sweetly into our ears, saying, "Give me your vineyard," men of principle and integrity must have the courage to say, "Not for sale."

But exactly how do we stand up and speak out for what we know to be right?

RESPECTFULLY HOLDING OUR OWN

We often struggle with how to respond to situations of compromise—whether in the workplace, community, or church. What does it mean to maintain integrity when you feel called to stand up for principle?

For example, many of us know that errors are being taught and practiced in our churches, or that injustice is being committed at the levels where we operate. However, in wanting to maintain our integrity, we manifest that integrity with a spirit that undermines what we're trying to accomplish.

In other words, sometimes the *how* of our approach creates more problems than the *what* for which we are standing. The truth has often been rejected not on its own merits but because of those who carry or proclaim it.

Here are a few things to consider when we are called upon to stand for principle or truth. As a mnemonic device, I would list them with P's.

1. The Power of Prayer

We must not speak out or act upon any issue until we pray earnestly about the wrong we intend to correct. Prayer softens the hearts of evil-doers. It also allows us to obtain wisdom from God as to the timing and approach we should adopt. Prayer makes us feel our own need. It prepares us to treat others the way we ourselves would want to be treated, were we in the situation of the people we now seek to correct.

We must ask the Lord to grant us wisdom as to how to effect corrections or changes through our witness (by voice, pen, or example). While praying for courage to stand for the truth and principle, let us ask the Lord to help us to be humble and courteous. Let us pray earnestly that the Lord will cause those we are trying to correct to see the light we have seen. Much more can be accomplished on our knees than through all the direct action, political pressures, and other manipulations that we may be capable of mustering.

2. The Power of Personal Example

Sometimes a godly life is itself a non-verbal way of speaking out against error or evil. This is particularly the case when others who are more capable than ourselves are addressing the issue and when our own lives are already speaking out against what we want to correct. In such instances, our lives can accomplish more than our words.

Our personal examples then augment or strengthen the work others are doing on the same issue. This approach is highlighted in Christ's treatment of Herod:

> "Christ might have spoken words to Herod that would have pierced the ears of the hardened king. He might have stricken him with fear and trembling by laying before him the full iniquity of his life, and the horror of his approaching doom. But Christ's silence was the severest rebuke that He could have given. Herod had rejected the truth spoken to him by the greatest of the prophets, and no other message was he to receive. Not a word had the Majesty of heaven for him."[54]

3. The Power of the Pen

While praying for a change and refuting error or evil by our personal example, we must also allow ourselves to be instruments of change. Those of us able to write should write. Those able to speak should speak. Those able to vote should make their voices heard. But by all means, we must be directly involved in the change we seek to see.

When we have to speak out with our voices and pens, we must be as gentle as we are firm. Sometimes the tone and spirit of our "speaking out" can undo all the good we seek to accomplish. For this reason, we must "convince, rebuke, exhort, *with all longsuffering*" (2 Timothy 4:2).

A godly life, combined with a gentle, submissive attitude, adds great force to our witness: "But in your hearts set apart Christ as Lord. Always be prepared to give an answer to everyone who asks you to give the reason for the hope that you have. *But do this with gentleness and respect*" (1 Peter 3:15, NIV).

On one hand, *gentleness* is a humble attitude that enables us to keep our volatile emotions in check. It is a calmness that prevents us from vitriolic and bitter words and actions. On the other hand, *respect* is to accord to the other person whatever rights we claim for ourselves. It would never allow us to look down on or put down those hold a differing view from us. Neither would respect allow us to call them names, hurl insulting epithets at them, or employ damaging insinuations toward them.

Also, although direct rebuke is sometimes necessary, the apostle Paul reminds us there are times when an appeal or entreaty is preferable. "Do *not rebuke* an older man, but *exhort* him as a father, younger men as brothers, older women as mothers, younger women as sisters, with all purity" (1 Timothy 5:1, 2).

4. The Power of Personal Involvement

When we are clear on what we should or shouldn't do; when we have prayerfully sought wisdom on the timing and the proper approach and spirit by which we should stand for what is right, we must act decisively. We must be actively involved to rectify the errors or ills.

About 2,000 years ago, our Lord Jesus transported us to the future, making us aware of what He would say to us on the day of reckoning. He would say to those of us we fail to act: "I was sick and in prison and you visited Me not." The question would then be asked of the Lord: "Lord, when did we see You hungry or thirsty or a stranger or naked or sick or in prison, and did not minister to You?" The resounding reply of Jesus is as much directed at us today as it would be to His professed followers two millennia ago: "Assuredly, I say to you, inasmuch as you did it to one of the least of these My brethren, you did it to Me" (Matthew 25:40–45).

We are not going to be held accountable just for the sin of commission but also for the sin of omission. The "elders and nobles of Jezreel" may not have actively participated in the murder of Naboth. However, to the extent that they refused to act, they were culpable.

It is not enough simply to say, "Let's pray about" or "Let the Lord take care" of the situation. Prayer is important, but prayers without principled actions will not change a wrong situation. Sometimes "prayer" alone is a camouflage for cowardice. Men of principle are men of action.

We need men like Nehemiah in the church today, not men who can pray and preach only, but men whose prayers and sermons are braced with firm and eager purpose. For his decided effort, the walls of ancient Jerusalem, which had lain in ruins for more than a hundred years, was rebuilt in just fifty-two days! Concerning this great reformer, we read:

> "The success attending Nehemiah's efforts shows what prayer, faith, and wise, energetic action will accomplish. Nehemiah was not a priest; he was not a prophet; he made no pretension to high title. He was a reformer raised up for an important time. It was his aim to set his people right with God. Inspired with a great purpose, he bent every energy of his being to its accomplishment. High, unbending integrity marked his efforts. As he came into contact with evil and opposition to right he took so determined a stand that the people were roused to labor with fresh zeal and courage. They could not but recognize his loyalty, his patriotism, and his deep love for God; and, seeing this, they were willing to follow where he led."[55]

Those who defy the culture of silence are people who take decided action to correct wrong. When these men of principle take a stand, when they speak up, when they act, it inspires others to join their rank.

5. The Power of Patience
After we've done all humanly possible at one end, we must be willing to wait. Sometimes, our actions may seem as if they are not bearing fruit, but with time the result will become evident.

In any case, God is on the throne, and He has His own timing. He may choose to change or remove some people from leadership. He may choose to send somebody from outside to come and aid our efforts. In short, God has a thousand ways to effect changes, of which we know nothing. Our role is simply to do what we're most capable of doing and leave the results in God's hands.

Patience allows us to see God work. This is why the Bible repeatedly urges us: "Be still, and know that I am God; I will be exalted among the nations, I will be exalted in the earth!" (Psalm 46:10). "Wait on the Lord; be of good courage, and He shall strengthen your heart; wait, I say, on the Lord!" (Psalm 27:14); "But those who wait on the Lord shall renew their strength; they shall mount up with wings like eagles, they shall run and not be weary, they shall walk and not faint" (Isaiah 40:31).

Through the years, whenever I have been discouraged by compromises in my own church and by God's apparent inaction, I have found the following comments by E. G. White (1827–1915) reassuring:

> "There is no need to doubt, to be fearful that the work will not succeed. *God is at the head of the work, and He will set everything in order.* If matters need adjusting at the head of the work, God will attend to that, and work to right every wrong. Let us have faith that God is going to carry the noble ship which bears the people of God safely into port."[56]

> "Jesus sees the end from the beginning. In every difficulty, He has His way prepared to bring relief. Our Heavenly Father has a thousand ways to provide for us of which we know nothing. Those who accept the one principle of making the service of God supreme, will find perplexities vanish and a plain path before their feet."[57]

> "Those who surrender their lives to His guidance and His service will never be placed in a position for which He has not made provision. Whatever our situation, if we are doers of His Word, we have a Guide to direct our way; whatever our perplexity, we have a sure Counselor; whatever our sorrow, bereavement, or loneliness, we have a sympathizing Friend."[58]

> "If I did not believe that God's eye is over His people, I could not have the courage to write the same things over and over again....God has a people whom He is leading and instructing."[59]

In short, being men and women of principle means that we must be willing to be instruments of change. Even if we are the only ones, we must act. And we must be willing, if need be, to pay the ultimate price for our principled position and action—however undeserved the injustice may be. Such were the experiences of Naboth and Christ.

PERSPECTIVE ON SENSELESS DEATHS

Naboth's death was totally undeserved. It was meaningless. It was an absurd, senseless murder. In this respect, Naboth's death is strikingly similar to the deaths of all innocent people. Consider the following examples—

- *Abel*—was murdered because "his works were evil and his brother's righteous."[60]

- *Zechariah*—was executed between the altar and the porch because of King Joash's ungratefulness.[61]

- *Uriah*—was deliberately set up by King David, thrust to the forefront of a battle and killed, because the king wanted to cover up his adulterous pregnancy with Uriah's wife Bathsheba.[62]

- *John the Baptist*—was senselessly beheaded, because of Herodias' grudge, a little girl's seductive dance, and Herod's drunken oath.[63]

- *Stephen*—was stoned to death for reminding his audience of their complicit involvement in the death of Christ.[64]

All these deaths, like Naboth's, were absurd—innocent people murdered for no crimes they had committed. And in these deaths, we see the many deaths that are similarly pointless and irrational—the Holocaust, past and present genocides, ethnic cleansings, racial lynchings, and other forms of hate murders.

How do we make sense of the absurd death of Naboth? How can the pointless deaths recorded in the Bible and witnessed in human history be significant to us?

I think the answer lies in another senseless death—the shameful death of our Lord Jesus Christ. And from the pointless death of Christ we look back and understand the absurd death of Naboth and the millions of other pointless human deaths.

From the parable Jesus told about a vineyard, it is evident that He saw Himself as the "beloved Son" who was murdered when His Father, the owner of the vineyard, sent Him to His vineyard:

> "Then the owner of the vineyard said, 'What shall I do? I will send my beloved son. Probably they will respect him when they see him.' But when the vinedressers saw him, they reasoned among themselves, saying, 'This is the heir. Come, let us kill him, that the inheritance may be ours.' So they cast him out of the vineyard and killed him. Therefore what will the owner of the vineyard do to them?" (Luke 20:13–15)

But the striking similarity between the story of Naboth and that of our Lord Jesus Christ goes beyond a mere reference to vineyards. When we read the Gospel accounts of the final events of Christ's life—from Gethsemane to Calvary—we discover a story far more disturbing than that of Naboth.

The New Testament accounts make clear that the enemies of Jesus had no legitimate reason to kill Him. Like Naboth's own, the trial of Jesus was a complete farce:

> "Now the chief priests and all the council sought testimony against Jesus to put Him to death, but found none. For many bore false witness against Him, but their testimonies did not agree. Then some rose up and bore false witness against Him, saying, 'We heard Him say, "I will destroy this temple made with hands, and within three days I will build another made without hands."' But not even then did their testimony agree. And the high priest stood up in the midst and asked Jesus, saying, 'Do You answer nothing? What is it these men testify against You?' But He kept silent and answered nothing. Again the high priest asked Him, saying to Him, 'Are You the Christ, the Son of the Blessed?'" (Mark 14:55–61)

Not only does the Gospel narrative reveal the ridiculous nature of the fabricated charges, it also paints a graphic picture of the steps that led to the crucifixion of Christ. When we go back and read again the passion narratives in the light of Naboth's death, we shall discover that his death points to the cross of Christ.

From Pilate, who handed Christ over to be crucified, to the soldier who watched Him die, the evidence shows that there was no legitimate reason why Christ should have been killed. He was innocent. Yet He was tortured and murdered, on the basis of a fabrication of lies. His cruel death was senseless.

Like Naboth, Christ was also the victim of an absurd death. In His shameful death on Calvary's cross, He took upon Himself the wounds, torture, suffering, and death of all victims of senseless death. In other words, the cold-blooded execution of Naboth and his sons, in all its absurdity and senselessness, pointed forward to the unjust death of Jesus Christ, who "humbled himself, and became obedient unto death, even the death of the cross" (Philippians 2:8).

And from the perspective at Calvary, from the shameful crucifixion on the cross, we can look back and see the light of Christ through Naboth's death—and every other senseless death throughout history and in the world today.

Today's Naboths should be encouraged by the fact that Jesus Himself trod this difficult path, leaving traces of His blood on its flints. Countless thousands have also passed by the same way. This knowledge—that others and Christ have traversed the same dark valley of suffering and death—should be comforting to us during times of our own trials and afflictions.

"Although it may seem that you are all alone here, yet you are not alone; for Christ is with you; you are in blessed company. You have the words coming down the line from prophets and apostles, to encourage you to steadfastness. Many of these holy men lost their lives for their faithfulness to God. If you suffer for the truth's sake, remember that this is no more than others have done before you."[65]

Yes, we are never alone in our suffering of injustice. Christ shares in our sorrow and pain. He identifies with our sufferings. One of the most beautiful sentiments recorded in the Bible is found in Isaiah, chapter 63, verse 9. It reads: "In all their affliction he was afflicted." It means that God sympathizes with His people in all their trials, hurt, and death.

In the book *The Desire of Ages*, arguably the best biography on the life of Christ, the author puts it this way:

"Through all our trials we have a never-failing Helper. He does not leave us alone to struggle with temptation, to battle with evil, and be finally crushed with burdens and sorrow. Though now He is hidden from mortal sight, the ear of faith can hear His voice saying, Fear not; I am with you. 'I am He that liveth, and was dead; and, behold, I am alive forevermore.' Revelation. 1:18. I have endured your sorrows, experienced your struggles, encountered your temptations. I know your tears; I also have wept. The griefs that lie too deep to be breathed into any human ear, I know. Think not that you are desolate and forsaken. Though your pain touch no responsive chord in any heart on earth, look unto Me, and live. 'The mountains shall depart, and the hills be removed; but My kindness shall not depart from thee, neither shall the covenant of My peace be removed, saith the Lord that hath mercy on thee.'" (Isa. 54:10)[66]

From Calvary's cross we have a better perspective on every episode of senseless suffering, violence, and death. And the realization that God is with us in our trials should give us strength to carry our heavy burdens:

"Do not depend upon human aid. Look beyond human beings to the One appointed by God to bear our griefs, to carry our sorrows, and to supply our necessities. Taking God at His word, make a beginning wherever you find work to do, and move forward with unfaltering faith. It is faith in Christ's presence that gives strength and steadfastness."[67]

ATTITUDE OF PATIENT SILENCE

There is a need for unwavering integrity in the world. This need was aptly captured a century ago in the insightful statement that inspired this book:

"The greatest want of the world is the want of men—men who will not be bought or sold, men who in their inmost souls are true and honest, men who do not fear to call sin by its right name, men whose conscience is as true to duty as the needle to the pole, men who will stand for the right though the heavens fall."[68]

In more recent times, a well-known and beloved Bible teacher has summarized what this lack of integrity entails:

THE WORLD NEEDS MEN...

who cannot be bought;
whose word is their bond;
who put character above wealth;
who possess opinions and a will;
who are larger than their vocations;
who do not hesitate to take chances;
who will not lose their individuality in a crowd;
who will be as honest in small things as in great things;
who will make no compromise with wrong;
whose ambitions are not confined to their own selfish desires;
who will not say they do it "because everybody else does it";
who are true to their friends through good report and evil report,
in adversity as well as in prosperity;
who do not believe that shrewdness, cunning, and hardheadedness
are the best qualities for winning success;
who are not ashamed or afraid to stand for the truth when it is unpopular;
who can say "no" with emphasis, although all the rest of the world says "yes."[69]

Naboth was a Bible character who could say "No" with emphasis and mean it. He turned down what seemed like an excellent business offer from King Ahab, declaring that his vineyard was "not for sale." Naboth was a man of honor who stood by his convictions without wavering.

The passage in 1 Kings 21 teaches us that a lot more is at stake in the seemingly ordinary decisions we make. In the vineyards entrusted to our care, we have a unique identity to preserve, the heritage of our fathers to cherish, and a spiritual integrity and loyalty to uphold. This is why our principles, values, and consciences should not be for sale.

The story of Naboth also teaches us that after we have stood up for what is right; after we have faithfully defended what is at stake, we must be willing to suffer the consequences of our principled decisions. If needs be, we must patiently suffer hurt or death, trusting our case with the righteous Judge.

I call this response to injustice *patient silence*. Unlike the cowardly silence of the "elders and nobles of the city of Jezreel," patient silence describes the demeanor of Naboths—those who stand for something and are willing to give up their lives for it.

The two words in the expression are calculated to emphasize the dual qualities of gentleness and meekness in the face of injustice. *Gentleness* is the active side of patient silence. It describes the manner in which we should treat others. *Meekness* is the passive component, depicting the proper response we should adopt when others mistreat us.

Gentleness and meekness reveal the inner fortitude of a principled person—one who will not be bought or sold. Thus understood, the expression *patient silence* combines resolute conviction and character with a winning grace of humility. Christ alone ever fully expressed this quality. He was meek and gentle, even when He suffered hurt. "He humbled Himself and became obedient to the point of death, even the death of the cross" (Philippians 2:8).

> "For to this you were called, because Christ also suffered for us, leaving us an example, that you should follow His steps: 'Who committed no sin, Nor was deceit found in His mouth'; who, when He was reviled, did not revile in return; when He suffered, He did not threaten, but committed Himself to Him who judges righteously."
> (1 Peter 2:21–23)

We are called to emulate His meekness and gentleness. Thus, the apostle Paul appealed to the Corinthian Christians "by the *meekness* and *gentleness* of Christ" (2 Corinthians 10:1). Christ Himself said, "Take my yoke upon you, and learn of me; for I am *meek* and *lowly* in heart: and ye shall find rest unto your souls." (Matthew 11:29)

Patient silence is the quality that enables us to hold on, no matter what. It is that which inspires us to be true to the "faith of our fathers," in spite of the consequences. And it is that character alone—itself, the result of a totally surrendered life to Christ—that enables us to forgive and be gracious to those who mistreat us because of our principled stance.

As we resolve, by the grace of God, not to be bought or sold, may we find encouragement in the words of Frederick William Faber's (1814–1863) classic hymn:

Faith of our fathers! Living still
In spite of dungeon fire, and sword,
O how our hearts beat high with joy
Whene'er we hear that glorious word.
Faith of our fathers! Holy faith!
We will be true to thee till death.

Our fathers, chained in prisons dark,
Were still in heart and conscience free;
How sweet would be their children's fate,
If they, like them, could die for thee!
Faith of our fathers! Holy faith!
We will be true to thee till death.

Faith of our fathers! We will love
Both friend and foe in all our strife,
And preach thee, too, as love knows how,
By kindly words and virtuous life.
Faith of our fathers! Holy faith!
We will be true to thee till death.

NOTES

53 Ephesians 1:14, NASB.

54 *The Desire of Ages*, p. 730.

55 E. G. White, *Prophet and King*, p. 675.

56 *Review and Herald*, September 20, 1892; *Selected Messages*, bk. 2, p. 30, emphasis mine.

57 *The Ministry of Healing*, p. 481.

58 *Ibid.,* pp. 248, 249.

59 *Selected Messages*, bk. 2, p. 397.

60 1 John 3:12; cf. Genesis 4; Hebrews 11:4.

61 Luke 11:51; cf. 2 Chronicles 24:17–22.

62 2 Samuel 11 and 12.

63 Mark 6:14–29; Matthew 14:1–12.

64 Acts 7:1–59.

65 *Historical Sketches of the Foreign Missions of the Seventh-day Adventists*, p. 197).

66 *The Desire of Ages*, p. 483.

67 *The Ministry of Healing*, p. 153.

68 E. G. White, *Education*, p. 57.

69 Charles Swindoll, *Living Above the Level of Mediocrity* (Dallas, TX: Word Publishing, 1989), pp. 107, 108.

PART 6
THEIR S

Though
Reflecti
From St

TORY

s and

ns

dents

"Those who read
   are those who lead.
But those who write
   keep the leaders right.
For silence is the crime
   by cowards of every time."

Samuel Koranteng-Pipim
*Ghanaian Scholar, Author
and Public Speaker, b. 1957*

CAMPUS REVIVAL

Historically, God has often launched major revival and reformation movements from public university campuses. For example, great movements were associated with John Wyclif at Oxford University, John Huss at the University of Prague, Martin Luther at the University of Wittenburg, John Calvin at the University of Geneva, John and Charles Wesley at Oxford University, and others.[70]

In our day, another spiritual revival is taking place on secular campuses in North America and around the world. CAMPUS is one of the centers of this grass-roots spiritual movement among young people, training students to be missionaries on their respective campuses.[71] These students are not only sacrificing one year of their education to volunteer as students on secular universities in Michigan but are also paying significant tuition and boarding fees to attend.[72]

The young people trained by CAMPUS have contributed immensely to the culture of excellence, sacrifice and commitment, and "can-do" spirit exhibited in a number of today's grass-roots youth movements.[73]

As explained in the Introduction of this book, in a real sense, the integrity described in *Not for Sale* is *about* the student missionaries at CAMPUS, and the challenge against the culture of silence is *to* them—and to all others, both young and old, who have been inspired by their selfless commitment.

The message of this book would be incomplete without hearing the voices of the student missionaries who inspired *Not for Sale*.

THOUGHTS FROM CURRENT STUDENTS

"What did you learn from this sermon on Naboth?"

I posed this question to our current (2008–2009) CAMPUS student missionaries after I shared with them the same sermon I had presented two days earlier at the Michigan Men of Faith meeting.

I asked the students to take a few minutes to reflect on the message and jot down thoughts sparked by the sermon—lessons learned, questions raised, prayers offered, and commitments they had made as a result of the sermon. After a few minutes, I asked each CAMPUS missionary to share with the class what they had written.

Words cannot adequately capture the solemnity and the mood of the class when each student read aloud his or her thoughts. The deep impact that their varied reflections had on me was the main impetus that inspired me to publish the sermon as a book.

Here are excerpts from their reactions—presented here in the order in which they were shared.

Being Firmly Grounded
Dora Boateng
Graduate of Case Western Reserve University, Ohio (Psychology, Pre-Med)

The message convicted me on the importance of being firmly grounded in my Christian beliefs and principles. Here are questions I asked myself:

1. Am I a Naboth (someone who sticks to principles)—or am I part of the councilmen of Jezreel?

2. In what situations have I acted as a Naboth, and when have I been a councilman, by keeping silent?

3. How can I be more grounded in what I believe or stand for amidst a world of chaos?

4. Like Ahab, what are the things of others that I "lust" after or covet?

5. As one of the "elders and nobles," how many opportunities have I allowed to pass me by?

May the Lord help me not to be swayed by popular opinions and to be firmly grounded in Him.

Selective Naboths

Cassandra Papenfuse
Graduate of University of Michigan (African Studies and International Health)

Here are my thoughts and commitments, based on the story of Naboth:

1. I need to be a stronger person. Too often I act as a "noble," simply following instructions for fear of rocking the boat. I need to fear more the repercussions of maintaining silence and less what the crowd will think.

2. My decisions and actions need to be less like Ahab (selfish and out of greed) and Jezebel (power and control hungry) and more like Naboth (loving obedience to God, and firm in understanding of my identity and purpose.) The former (model of Ahab and Jezebel) is dangerous and leads to destruction.

3. Godly women wield tremendous influence for good. But women like Jezebel—those who usurp for themselves roles other than what God has given them—cause havoc. Though women are smart, we should be careful not to use our intelligence or position for selfish gain.

4. I see myself sometimes as a "selective Naboth." On certain issues, I won't be bought or sold, but on other issues I can be weak and "break" under pressure. I want to be a real Naboth—one who knows my Lord and His will so closely that I will do nothing less than stand on His side, no matter what storm comes.

5. Like the "elders and nobles," all too often we confuse the command to be obedient to authority with the command to be obedient to God. This is so dangerous! In all things, I want to be clear on God's ways, so that I will be obedient to authority only when authority is in line with God.

Not Settling for Less

David Park

Student, University of Maryland (Electrical Engineering)

The message on 1 Kings 21 is a sobering one—especially the roles
played by Naboth and the elders and nobles. Standing for truth,
as God calls us to do, raises serious thought questions for me:

WHO am I, and am I willing to die for my convictions?

WHAT are the things in my life that are "not for sale?"

WHEN the time comes that justice is required, will I call out sin by
its right name, or (like Herod) compromise because of "those who sat?"
(Matthew 14:9).

WHERE might be places in my life that God has put me to stand for truth?

WHY do I believe what I believe?

HOW do I plan to go about preparing to meet the day when my integrity
and virtue will be challenged?

These questions will take more than an hour, a day, or perhaps even
months to answer. They require deep soul-searching and prayer.
May the Lord give us the courage to refuse settling for anything less
than pure, absolute, and complete truth.

Learning Silence

Rob Mosher

Graduate Student, Michigan State University (Computer Science)

The thing that strikes me most from this study is the importance of not being silent when something demands to be spoken against. This is brought out clearly in the conduct of the elders and nobles.

It may seem odd to so strongly condemn the elders and nobles. After all, they were not the principal architects of this villainy. Why then should those of us who sympathize with and condone the Ahabs and Jezebels of the world need a much stronger and more personal rebuke?

The elders and nobles have the power to cause change. Without their complicit will or indifference, the villains of the world would be powerless. And it is as them that, if we compromise, we take the risk of becoming Ahabs and Jezebels, so that we no longer take notice when we are in the wrong.

It seems we are taught to be silent in little ways throughout our life. Certain decisions may not be worth the argument. Questions in lectures are treated dismissively. Eventually, it becomes a habit to keep any disagreements within ourselves.

Further, we do not understand the importance of our beliefs. We don't know why we hold them, how they bring strength, and thus we don't know precisely what they are. So when they are challenged, we have no defense against attacks, and both the biblical and the new may seem equally good. Or we may know we should hold to the biblical, but we can't say why we must maintain it—we are unable to and afraid to articulate our viewpoint.

Certainly, standing up against wrong—being unwilling to sell our integrity— takes courage. But more so, it takes a knowledge of what we stand for and a deep appreciation for how it has impacted our lives and the lives of those around us. We need a conviction of what is right before we will find any courage to stand up for it.

We need faith—a faith so strong that we can speak as the three Hebrew boys, standing with assurance that God will defend us, and standing unwavering, though it may cost us our lives.

What Do I Stand For?

Brennen Varneck
Rock-Climbing Instructor, Alberta, Canada

I will sell myself out when I do not know who I am. Naboth knew who he was and for what he stood. He ended up dying for his faith, because he would not sell himself, his identity, or his purpose.

The people who killed Naboth also knew what they wanted and for what they stood. They were also fearless in moving forward in action matching their conviction.

Both Naboth and his enemies died. Not at the same time, but eventually, they died.

In the life to come Naboth will be rewarded with everlasting life in the presence of God for his faithfulness to the Word of God. At the same time, Ahab and Jezebel will be condemned and will receive their just punishment.

Both Naboth and his enemies lived. But they lived two different kinds of lives.

Naboth lived with freedom, with a light conscience, with no worries, and with no wants. He lived joyfully in every moment God gave him.

Ahab and Jezebel lived with burdens, with guilt, with that worm eating at their brain that continually told them, "You want more"—they were never satisfied.

The question that faces me is: "What do I stand for?" Will I live for God or for myself? I choose God.

"Choose you this day whom ye will serve; ...but as for me and my house, we will serve the LORD" (Joshua 24:15).

The Vineyard of Purpose
Michel Lee
Student, Stanford University, California (Pre-Med)

At first glance, it was *just* a piece of land. What is the significance of refusing to give up one's land—does this even merit mention in the Old Testament? And why risk one's life for a small plot of grapevines? The answer is that Naboth knew *why* he treasured and guarded his ancestral land in Jezreel. He knew what he stood for, and *thus* he was able to face death rather than compromise.

In contrast to the unwavering Naboth, the elders and nobles didn't protest the condemnation and death of Naboth, because they didn't know what they stood for, despite being God's chosen people. Isn't it sad that the *majority* of people didn't take a definite stance on the day of Naboth's stoning? It doesn't sound too much different from the silent majority in modern-day genocides, or even the American public, so easily swayed by a sleek political pitch and other superficial appeals to emotion. Humanity has sold its vineyards over and over again.

Yet I wonder if *I* myself truly cling to my professed beliefs, my Eternal Father. Or am I merely "bold and radical"—whatever that means!—because everyone else around me is, and I feel comfortable being radical? (What an oxymoron!) When the time comes for us to be truly radical, I wonder if we who profess to be God's last-day people will stand. Does my needle always, *always* point to the pole?

Every once in a while, someone preaches a sermon or gives a Bible study on God's purpose for our lives. I'm bemused every time this topic is broached, but every time my intentions to ponder my purpose quickly dissolve, and I return to my usual routine.

There might be two reasons for this: 1) I already know what my purpose is, or 2) I just don't care enough. Admittedly, I'm inclined to choose the latter. Now *that* troubles me. The story of Naboth pricks my heart, because I'm committing the same damning error as did the elders and nobles.

This is my problem: I don't know Jesus. To study and meditate upon Christ's life, character, and most important, His mission—now *that* would impart an unchangeable purpose to my life. This is my prayer—that I come to know Christ to the point of dying, because I refuse to sell that which He has appointed to me.

Missed Opportunities
Jonathan Martin
Graduate of Sierra College, California (Pre-Med)

Silence kills. Inactivity kills. Waiting to perform a known duty is to say
No to that duty. The story of Naboth's death is really the story of how well-
intentioned people allow themselves to do things they would otherwise
never do. It is the summary of missed opportunities to do good in my life,
of letting others speak while I remain silent for fear of not knowing what
to say or do.

Had I been in the crowd that day, there's a good chance I would have
waited for someone to say something, and then I'd support them. I would
get more and more anxious as I saw nothing happen and that a stoning
was inevitable. But instead of screaming, "Stop," I probably would have
fled and internalized the anguish in some corner of the city. It's a horrible
thought; it's not what I want my life to end up being—a continual fleeing
from failed rescue attempts and unfulfilled duties, of constantly going into
battle unready.

To save Naboth, I must learn to act decisively. God provides the power
and the opportunities, but they must be acted upon in order for their work
to be accomplished. This semester I will encounter many Naboths—
opportunities that cry for help and will be forever gone once they pass.
They will come at inopportune moments—times when the current will
be pressing against what ought to be done. If I allow myself, through
slackness of time, to be unprepared to help, or if I allow circumstances
to determine my course, I will be guilty of betraying these Naboths.

Killing Naboth—Again and Again
Kayla Piña
Graduate of Harvard University, Massachusetts (Sociology)

God is merciful. Every time I've betrayed His trust, He puts the desire to
be faithful into my heart again. But as I let time pass, becoming busy here
and there, and do not take time to prepare and strengthen my mind and my
decisions and convictions with Scripture and prayer, I come up to difficult
situations, and—over and over again—I kill Naboth. I sacrifice God's truth

and put others' salvation at risk because of my love of convenience, my ignorance, lack of discipline, and fear of the world.

I'm guilty of having "killed Naboth" again and again, especially during my four years of college. I distinctly remember particular classes that I left, feeling upset because I had opportunities to speak for truth and righteousness but said nothing: Intro to Sociology, Portuguese, Christian Literature, Residential Segregation, Social Theory, Psychology, and others. And I remember at least one conversation I had with a God-fearing friend in my sophomore year. After sharing my frustrations about one of my classes, he counseled that I should take that frustration as an example and study those topics further in the Bible so it never would happen again. But I didn't, and it happened again and again.

Every time I'm reminded of how many people, especially people who will become influential members of society, could have heard biblical truth but didn't because of one unfaithful, ignorant, so-called Christian, I feel sick.

Lord, forgive me. I don't want to dishonor You anymore. I don't want my heart to harden to the Holy Spirit. I don't want to see more opportunities pass by to stand up for righteousness and truth. How can this weakness and ignorance be removed from me? I know You have given me Your Word—Lord, give me the desire and strength to sacrifice *all* that is necessary to know, love, and share Your Word. Give me the desire and strength to live according to Your direction, even if I don't understand or see clearly at first. Wash away my sins, Lord, according to Your mercy, and help me to sin no more. Help me, Lord. I want to be a Christian—like Jesus, with His mind. Help me to learn. Help me to be faithful.

I see the need for men and women who will not be bought or sold. Make me that kind of woman, Lord: godly, of integrity, unmovable in the Word of God, that I, with other godly people, may help to hasten Jesus' coming and honor and vindicate Your name throughout the universe.

Teach me to think and not to be a mere reflector of other men's thoughts.

Teach me not to take any situation for granted and to remember that even one small or seemingly meaningless situation or act may have eternal consequences.

REFLECTIONS FROM PAST STUDENTS

Graduates from the one-year CAMPUS Missionary Training Program develop skills and a passion and commitment to minister to their fellow young people, especially students on public university campuses. Though they move on to different locations and vocations—whether as students, young professionals, or full-time ministry personnel—graduates from the Missionary Training Program continue to be connected with the work at CAMPUS.

Thus, at the same time that the current group of student missionaries was invited to share their thoughts on the "Not for Sale" sermon, some past CAMPUS missionaries were also asked to do the same. Here are a few reflections from them. Their thoughts also fueled the impetus to publish the sermon as a book.

I'm Not for Sale
Sikhululekile Hlatshwayo
Graduated from Wellesley College, Massachusetts (French and Biological Chemistry). Served as a CAMPUS missionary 2006–2007. Currently on CAMPUS staff.

This message struck me as a call to be principled. Some things, we must be unwilling to give up, no matter what we are offered in exchange—such as God's unique call on your life (vis-a-vis the specific land allocated to Naboth's family). There may be more enticing offers out there, but that doesn't matter. I'm not for sale.

Back home [in Africa], many girls would trade their bodies for school tuition or for some spending money from sugar daddies. I remember my mother telling my sisters and me not to sell ourselves. Young women are selling themselves for the sake of a relationship (that's not even worth their time). Young men are selling themselves for temporary pleasure. In response to this message, I can hear a principled young person telling his or her boyfriend/girlfriend, "Honey, I'm not for sale."

The idea of a sale signifies trading in one thing for another. In that sense, it becomes all-pervasive—what am I trading my time for; i.e., what do I *spend* my time doing? If time is our most valuable asset, then misusing it is selling ourselves short. Young people wouldn't waste time on unproductive video games, useless television watching, aimless web surfing—if they are not for sale!

I think the problem is that we put the wrong price tag on ourselves. We're selling ourselves cheap, because we don't realize our true value. Naboth knew that his value was determined by God. He was worth no more, and no less. The serpent convinced Eve that God undervalued her—that she was worth more than what God thought she was worth. On the flip side, I'm tempted to wonder sometimes if I'm even worth what God seems to think I'm worth—to wonder whether I'm too unworthy to be accepted by God. And with these thoughts, the devil tries to keep us from coming to God.

Whether we think God underestimates us or overestimates us, the result is the same—we're putting ourselves up for sale. If only we just had a right understanding of our identity—the identity and value God places on us!

Jesus had a right understanding of His identity, and He could not be bought by Satan in the wilderness of temptation. In the final hours of His life, Herod tried to bribe Him to perform some miraculous tricks in order to secure His freedom, but Jesus' silence in the courtroom declared, "I'm not for sale."

I want to say with Jesus, "I'm not for sale!"

"What good will it be for a man if he gains the whole world, yet forfeits his soul? Or what can a man give in exchange for his soul?...You were not redeemed with corruptible things, like silver or gold,... but with the precious blood of Christ, as of a lamb without blemish and without spot." (Matthew 16:26, NIV; 1 Peter 1:18, 19 NKJV)

Christ, the Trading Factor
Josephine Elia
Graduated from Massachusetts Institute of Technology (MIT). Served as a CAMPUS Missionary 2007–2008. Currently pursuing Ph.D. degree in Chemical Engineering at Princeton University.

"But what things were gain to me, those I counted loss for Christ. Yea doubtless, and I count all things but loss for the excellency of the knowledge of Christ Jesus my Lord: for whom I have suffered the loss of all things, and do count them but dung, that I may win Christ" (Philippians 3:7, 8).

Paul said, in the book of Philippians, that he went through a process whereby the definitions of gains and losses were transformed in his life. In fact, it was quite a revolutionary transformation. What he counted as gains before, including honor, privileged birth, education—which he listed in the earlier verses of chapter 3—he now counted as losses. He also implied that some things he did not regard as gains before, he now counted as rewards. What happened? Christ happened. And when Christ enters into one's life, some redefining takes place.

The question for us today is, How do we perceive gains and loses? Is Christ a factor in those categorizations?

The story of Naboth recounts the fate of a man not willing to sell a piece of himself to anything that compromised his relationship with God. In his system of thought, there had to be certain classifications that divided gains from losses, thus informing his decision to turn down Ahab's seemingly innocent offer. The choice was between money and a good personal relationship with the king and all the advantages that offered—and keeping the inheritance of his family that was given by God.

He chose to keep his land, meaning that he saw Ahab's offer as inferior to what he already had. Where did Naboth get the idea that his land was more precious than Ahab's offer? What was the factor that defined his concept of gains and losses? It was God—God was his reference point.

We may experiment with a hypothetical Naboth who doesn't have God as his reference point. Instead, he has something else occupying this place, say, himself. For this hypothetical Naboth, accepting Ahab's offer means an elevation in social status and perhaps an increase in wealth if Ahab's offer is high enough. A possible inconvenience would perhaps be moving his family and belongings to a new place, but if that doesn't bother him, it would not be counted as a loss.

Another reference point might be his family. If this were the case, upon receiving Ahab's offer, he would then consult his family and perhaps determine a system of voting in the family discussion. Depending on the result, he could then either turn down the king's offer or accept it. The gains and losses would be defined by a consensus of the family members.

What is the point of these hypothetical situations? It's that Naboth's reference point will determine how he will define what things are gains and what things are losses. It is the same with us today.

Whether we realize it or not, our decisions are guided by what we derive from a certain reference point. Companies and organizations have a list, implicit or explicit, of non-negotiable conditions. If something does not go along with their values and mission, the company doesn't strike a deal, even though someone else may say there is nothing wrong with it. This central value defines every decision and action of the organization.

Christians must have a single reference point in all aspects of life. God must be a factor in deciding what Christians call gains and losses. It is one thing to call myself a Christian and acknowledge that there is a God who oversees the universe—it is another thing to let Him enter into my world and reshuffle my priorities. If we are totally His, then all of our definitions, perceptions, and views must be derived from the fact that God is God and that I am His child. Is God a factor when I think about my choices? Is God's gain my gain, and His loss my loss?

Soon we will come upon a time where our priorities will be tested. When I read Naboth's story, I think of the persecutions that will soon befall upon us—the moments of crisis when we may be trapped in a well-covered conspiracy, just like Naboth. In these moments of panic, will I stand true or sell out?

The Bible says, "Yea, and all that will live godly in Christ Jesus shall suffer persecution" 2 Timothy 3:12. Persecution is a surety. We will have to choose to pledge allegiance to money or to God, to governing powers or to God, to family member or to God, to our own life or to God. If God is still for sale at that point, there is no chance of making it through.

It is about time that "putting God first" stops being a cliché and becomes an uncompromising reality in our lives and in His church. Jesus has to be number one on our non-negotiable list. He simply is NOT for sale. Some of us still put Him on sale, though for a very high price. We put Him in the back of the store, in very nice and expensive packaging. Some of us put Him in the display window of our shop. Some of us put Him in the bargain section. And Lord help us, some of us put Him in our garage sales.

Our definitions of gains and losses are radically different from the world's definitions. This difference is as radical as being joyful in the midst of persecution, such as the early church experienced. "After these things the word of the Lord came unto Abram in a vision, saying, Fear not, Abram: I am thy shield, and thy exceeding great reward" Gen 15:1. To lose all and gain only Christ, is to gain an exceeding great reward. May the Lord help us to count our gains and losses exactly as God counts His.

No Excuse

Thando Malambo

Chemistry student at Harvard University. Served as a CAMPUS Missionary 2007–2008.

As I read over the "mock" trial and murder of Naboth, I found myself cringing! "Please tell me that someone will stand up, please tell me that someone, *anyone*, will refuse to stand idly by while so great an injustice is inflicted on one who is least deserving of it."

But the only voices raised were those condemning Naboth to a cruel death. It's unbelievable, and more so because of the involvement of the "unnamed individuals"—the elders and nobles. They knew that Naboth was innocent and that he had done nothing to merit death. They fully understood what they were doing.

Yet they allowed themselves to be silent accomplices to the brutal murder of an innocent man. How can that be? What kind of wretchedness or inner struggle drives someone to the point of committing such a hideous crime against God and against humanity?

Were they trying to save face? Were they afraid of Jezebel? Did they not have guts enough to stand for the right against all earthly authority and pressure? Did they love their lives and reputations more than they loved God? What reason could possibly be justification enough for going along with the murder of an innocent and godly man? The same questions could be asked of those who murdered Christ.

I don't understand it. Matter of fact, I refuse to understand it. It is heart sickening—greatly disturbing. Yet it forces me to ask myself the question, "Are my own hands defiled with blood? Have not I myself been a silent accomplice to evil? How many times have I lied by my silence or omission? How many opportunities to speak out against evil have I left unimproved?"

But I think there is a deeper aspect, a greater evil—the world is full of men and women who are dying for want of knowledge of God. Have I, having full access to this knowledge, dared to share it with all? Or have I hesitated and thus potentially "killed" an innocent one who could have been saved?

I could enumerate countless examples. But the point remains: I'm deeply convicted. If I am going to belong to God at all, I must, by necessity, be wholly His. I must be bound by no earthly ties. Self, and all self-interest, must die! I must be firmly and unwaveringly committed to duty, no matter the cost, no matter the consequences.

In the words of one of my favorite quotes: "To stand in defense of truth and righteousness when the majority forsake us, to fight the battles of the Lord when champions are few, this will be our test."

Truly, "The greatest want of the world is the want of men...who will not be bought or sold," men and women who will fearlessly do the right, no matter what, men and women who will dare to go against the grain.

I want to be just such a young woman. There is no excuse for my not being—none whatsoever.

The Highest Bidder
Amy Lee Sheppard
Graduated from the University of Michigan. Served as a CAMPUS Missionary 2007–2008. Currently a graduate student, studying Law at the University of Virginia.

"The greatest want of the world is the want of men—men who will not be bought or sold, men who in their inmost souls are true and honest, men who do not fear to call sin by its right name, men whose conscience is as true to duty as the needle to the pole, men who will stand for the right though the heavens fall" (*Education*, p. 57).

As a child enrolled in church school, I remember memorizing the famous quote above and having no idea what it meant. I had no idea what it was talking about, but it had nonetheless been seared into my memory for reflection over the years to come.

Now, as a slightly more mature young adult, I realize the weight of these words. The first thing that occurred to me while reflecting on this quote in light of the story of Naboth was the question, Why would a person allow themselves to be bought or sold in the first place? The United States outlawed the sale of people as goods almost a century and a half ago, by abolishing slavery. If a person can be bought or sold, she has no power for self-determination and cannot make her own decisions as far as what work to do, where to live, or how to spend her time. She is a slave—she is not free.

Could it be that the greatest want of the world is the want of men who are free? Men who are not bound by the temptations, allurements, pleasures, and appetites of sin? That would explain why they would not be afraid to call it by its right name. Sin has no power over them, nothing with which to blackmail them.

A person, then, who cannot be bought or sold is the only person who is truly free. Naboth was free—free from bondage to anyone and free from sin.

On further contemplation, this idea goes even deeper, because the reality is that we already have been bought. Paul tells us twice, "ye are bought with a price" (1 Corinthians 6:20; 1 Corinthians 7:23). If we have already been bought for a price, why then can't we be sold? Bought out? If we have been bought, are we really free?

The answer to the first question—why we cannot be sold—is this: No one can pay the price. Peter tells us that "ye know that ye were not redeemed with corruptible things, as silver and gold, from your vain conversation received by tradition from your fathers but with the precious blood of Christ..." 1 Peter 3:18, 19. The cost to buy out a child of God is the blood of Jesus—the blood of the One in whom "dwelleth the fullness of the Godhead bodily" Colossians 2:9. Jesus set the price that His children are worth—His life. Nothing in the world can match this price.

The second reason extends from this understanding: If we were bought, we have no power to decide to sell ourselves. So really, we are not free. Yes, we are free from sin. Praise the Lord! But we are not free. Paul says in Romans 6:18, "Being then made free from sin, ye became the servants of righteousness."

We have no chance for autonomy. We are always going to be an agent of someone (Romans 6:20, 22), either of God, who valued us with the priceless gift of Jesus—or of Satan, who will buy us for the lowest price he can. Our freedom comes in this choice—who we get to serve.

Taking all these things into consideration, I realize, both on a rational and emotional level, that the story of Naboth makes sense. In economic terms, Jesus is the highest bidder, *He was not only willing to pay the price, He already did*. Naboth knew that this is Who he belonged to. Why would he want to serve anyone who valued him any less?

Maybe this is why it is the greatest want of the world. The greatest want of the world is not so much a want of men. Rather, it is a want of what those men represent. The greatest want of the world is for men who realize that there is something greater than the world. And a person who consistently lives a life not selling out to the things of this life is the strongest evidence in favor of the fact that there is something that will fulfill that desire. Even more, it is the strongest evidence that there is *Someone* who will fulfill that need.

As in daily contact with "the world," I realize what I've just discussed is the lens through which I must evaluate every decision I make—the rule by which I live my life. I am not my own. I cannot do anything, say anything, be anything, that would sell me out from the Master I love serving. Because in so doing, not only do I take away the only way I have to escape the slavery of this world, I also deprive those around me from an argument that it is possible to be set free—that we are worth something. And not just some thing—everything.

This thought is humbling and scary, because not only does the world want men and women for this reason, God *needs* men and women for this reason. I know that I am not made of the "stuff" of Naboth, Joseph, Daniel, Elijah or Elisha, Moses, or Paul—men such as this quote describes. I probably fall in line more often with the elders and nobles. While rationally it may make sense not to sell out for the world, temptation still rears its head, and the thought "just this one time" often sneaks in. But the rest of the quote encourages me. These men were not originally made of the right "stuff" either. None of us are. It is not accidental—and not something with which we are born. The same act of surrender which signals my acceptance of Jesus as master of my life rather than Satan sets me on the path to learn how to be like the Master I'm serving. It's true. I am not made of what it takes to be a person of such qualities. No one is. But Jesus makes us into those people.

My prayer, then, is that in all things, I may do nothing to sell myself out, because no price is worth it, and I am not my own to sell. I pray for help from God, that my life will be for those in the world around me an encouragement, showing that there is something worth more than this life has to offer and Someone worth living for—and that my life will spur them to enter into this kind of experience as well.

A Wake-Up Call

Sebastien Braxton

*Graduated from Eastern Michigan University with a degree in finance.
Served as a CAMPUS Missionary 2003–2004. Currently the Director of
STRIDE (Student Training and Resource Institute for Discipleship and
Evangelism), Cambridge, Massachusetts.*

I would highlight four things that moved me in the sermon about Naboth.

1. Courteous, But Firm. The first was the combination of Naboth's firmness, yet courteousness. Typically, when we are challenged to stand up against injustice, compromise, a lowering of the standards, or an attack upon our integrity, we are firm—but we have lost that grace of courtesy—the ability to refuse the invitation to compromise without rejecting the individual tempting us to do so. We need to stand for the right uncompromisingly, yet remain calm, meek, and winsome.

I believe Jesus possessed this rare ability. It was said that that He had "commanding dignity with the winning grace of humility" or "all absorbing devotion to God with tender love for man." "He manifested unyielding firmness with gentleness."[74] I believe this is a key component often left out by those who are committed to truth. The truth has often been rejected, not on its own merits, but because of its carriers.

It has become my prayer that I would not only burn with a zealousness for the glory of God and His truth but also defend it, preach it, and live it in such a way that the observing universe may clearly see that the objection is not against my own marred character but against the truth.

The great Protestant reformer Martin Luther displayed the rare qualities of firmness and courteousness on April 18, 1521, when he appeared at the Diet of Worms. During that trial, when the imperial officer pointed to Luther's writings and demanded that the young reformer answer whether or not he would retract the positions advanced therein, Luther replied:

"Seeing that it is a question which concerns faith and the salvation of souls, and in which the word of God, the greatest and most precious treasure either in heaven or earth, is involved, *I should act imprudently were I to reply without reflection. I might affirm less than the circumstance demands, or more than truth requires, and so sin against this saying of Christ*: 'Whosoever shall deny Me before men, him will I also deny before My Father which is in heaven.' [Matthew 10:33]. For this reason I entreat your imperial majesty, *with all humility* to allow me time, that I may answer without offending against the word of God."[75]

Commenting on Luther's reply, the author of the *The Great Controversy* writes:

"In making this request, Luther moved wisely. His course convinced the assembly that *he did not act from passion or impulse. Such calmness and self-command, unexpected in one who had shown himself bold and uncompromising, added to his power*, and enabled him afterwards to answer with prudence, decision, wisdom, and dignity that surprised and disappointed his adversaries, and rebuked their insolence and pride."[76]

In the 1 Kings 21 passage, Naboth displayed the same kind of calmness, when he firmly explained to Ahab why the vineyard was not for sale.

2. **The Faith of Our Fathers.** Naboth's explanation that the inheritance of his fathers forbade him from selling the vineyard deeply moved me. In a sense, the faith of his ancestors (those who had held faithful to God before him) and that of his progeny (who would come after him), lay in Naboth's hands. It was not only his integrity at stake but that of all those who had been faithful before him. His compromise would be theirs.

To think of the many martyrs who sealed their testimonies with their blood to the truth of righteousness by faith! To think of the pioneers who, through a disappointment unparalleled in history, moved humbly to prophesy again! To think of those preachers who spent their lives in proclaiming Christ and His Word! To think of all these—and so many more—makes selling the inheritance unthinkable. For I would be saying that their lives, sacrifices, and testimonies were in vain. Their fidelity was only followed by my infidelity, their commitment by my lack thereof, or their devotion by my betrayal. They thought not of themselves but of those before and after them.

Luther said to Melanchthon, as to why he should not go with him to the Diet of Worms, "If I do not return, and my enemies put me to death, continue to teach, and stand fast in the truth. Labor in my stead.... If you survive, my death will be of little consequence."

Naboth teaches me that a lot more is at stake when I'm tempted to betray or compromise the faith of our fathers.

3. **Nobles and Elders.** It was upon this point that I began to see the parallels between Naboth and Christ. Though it was the religious leaders behind the conspiracy of Christ's death, the actual call for His blood and crucifixion came from the unnamed crowd. They were the ones who were really guilty. This made me think of the times that I did not stand, because I was unnamed. Often we do not brook the tide of injustice, due to our lack of titles or apparent power and influence.

As the laity, we must seek God's forgiveness, for we have consented unto the death of our Lord in the person of those whom we have not defended, though we knew they were innocent. We have consented in those truths we did not defend as they were cast down from pulpits and Bible study groups. In these, we find our Innocent Savior condemned and His blood on our hands. As we grasp that there is a cause bigger than ourselves, we should become self-forgetful.

In the story of Naboth, the nobles and elders were the last means of staying this conspiracy and injustice. In this sense, we are not the bottom but the apex of the mechanism God has set in place to stay injustice within the Church. Thus, it becomes a challenge to move, as the maidservant of Naaman, though unnamed, to proclaim the truth out of love for it, humanity, and our Master.

4. **Labeled an Enemy.** I think this is the nuts and bolts of why the unnamed nobles and elders do not stand for the right though the heavens fall. No one wants to be a troublemaker. No one wants enemies. But as the sermon forcefully pointed out, in the light of the great controversy, it is not only about choosing our friend but our enemy. By choosing Christ, Truth, and Love, we have automatically declared Satan, error, and anything against love, to be our enemy. This fear is a subtle attempt to serve two masters.

Fundamentally, it is really about us getting over ourselves. Who are we to hold back the truth? Who are we to stand in the way of the truth? If we are not gathering with Christ, then we are scattering. Either we are whole-hearted Christians or none at all. God is looking for hundred-percenters. It is the first and great commandment in the Law to love Christ with *all—100 percent*.

If loving Christ causes me to be declared an enemy, then so be it. For I am a friend of God. If God be for us, who can be against us? Thus, I have made a commitment and made it my prayer to never allow my fear of being labeled to motivate my decision to speak up or not, but to be motivated simply by Christ and His truth. Jesus told us, "Blessed are you when men shall revile you and persecute you, and say all manner of evil against you falsely for my sake. Rejoice and be exceeding glad: for great is your reward in heaven, for so persecuted they the prophets which were before you" (Matthew 5:11, 12).

This message is a wake-up call to youth and leaders around the world. We cannot claim innocence as we sit idly by, not stemming the moral decadence within the church. We must no longer permit the "Naboths" of our day, who are holding the inheritance of our fathers, to be stoned by those who do not have the moral rectitude to admit their wrongs, humble themselves before the truth, and defend Christ in His Word.

This has gone on for too long, and by God's grace, I pray that the Lord strengthen and embolden me to stand and be counted, even if alone. I believe this is what the world and the church awaits in these perilous times.

A POETIC SUMMARY: A POEM ON THE STORY

I got to know Lance Landall of New Zealand about a year ago via the Internet. He was reared as a Christian but wandered away from his faith and his Lord, but slowly returned and later became seriously committed to the Christian walk and his faith. A studious Bible student, Lance shares his faith through rhymed poems (see his website: http://www.poetrywithamission.co.nz/poems.html). Lance penned the following poem after he read my sermon "Not for Sale."

NOT FOR SALE

Remember Daniel? He couldn't be bought or sold—wasn't for sale
Regardless of persecution, the threat of death, or jail.
No, he didn't have his price, but rather, stood firm and true,
And only that which was right, chose to think, proclaim, pursue.

Likewise Naboth.

Daniel was a man of principle—he had integrity,
He couldn't be bribed, he always acted ethically.
He was not afraid of man, nor one to go with the flow,
He kept his word—that is, his "yes" meant "yes;" his "no" meant "no."

Likewise John the Baptist.

Daniel had the courage to stand alone—speak up, speak out;
When it came to right or wrong, he chose right—wasn't in doubt.
He was true to His Master, true to himself—trustworthy,
A man, a real man, who followed his Master faithfully.

Likewise Stephen.

When push came to shove, Daniel was there, a man for his time,
His daily witness had a heavenly rhythm and rhyme.
He refused to compromise, went by his conscience, not his peers,
And right throughout his life remained the same, Scripture declares.

Likewise Esther.

Are *you* a Daniel, who can't be bought or sold—not for sale
Regardless of persecution, the threat of death, or jail?
Do you stand firm, stand alone, speak up, speak out, remain true,
And only that which is right, choose to think, proclaim, pursue?

Are you another Luther?

Or do you—via silence and inaction—simply aid ill,
And via cowardice or fear, effectively prophecy fulfil?
Oh, how tragic it would be, should you be aiding heresy,
Due to self-preservation, or acting misguidedly.

Does Judas or Pilate come to mind?

It could be said—that in times of crisis—such is treachery,
For such a time is not a time for acting selfishly.
Rather, it's time to be a Daniel and let God's will prevail,
To make it known to all, that come what may, you're not for sale.

Like Mary, the mother of Jesus, who let God's will prevail.

What the world's in great need of, more than anything else, today,
Is men who won't be bought or sold, men who're loyal—don't betray.
Yes, men who aren't afraid to call sin by its rightful name,
Men and women—who despite the cost—will shout in heaven's name.

Like Nehemiah.

Whose conscience is as true to duty as the needle to the pole,
And who—(praise God)—are honest and true in their inmost soul.
Men and women, who don't stand idly by, but dare to speak,
When others attack God's truth, or such truth attempt to tweak.

Noah, Daniel, Job—fitting examples of righteousness—(Eze. 14:14, 20).

Yes, who won't be intimidated by jeers, lies, or threats,
For any who are, both error and its source, aids and abets.
It's time to be a hero, to follow the steps of those
Who because they weren't for sale, the same path as their Lord chose.

Remember Jeremiah?

Let me ask you again: Are you a Daniel—not for sale
Regardless of persecution, the threat of death, or jail?
Are you a "watchman"—one who's not asleep, but wide awake,
Who the "Faith of our Fathers" won't betray, nor truth forsake?

Are you another Paul (2 Cor. 11:23-28)?

In an age of universal deceit, telling the truth, friend,
Is a revolutionary act—that says, I won't bend.
In other words, it takes a Daniel, who'll let God prevail,
And who'll declare to all, that come what may, they're NOT FOR SALE

This is the challenge for Elijahs in the world of Ahabs and Jezebels,
Yes, Elijahs, in whom the Holy Spirit strongly dwells.

By Lance Landall
For more about the author and his "Poems With a Mission,"
check his website: http://www.poetrywithamission.co.nz/index.html.

NOTES

70 For more on this, see E. G. White, *The Great Controversy* (Boise, Idaho: Pacific Press, 1911), pp. 79-264.

71 CAMPUS, the Center for Adventist Ministry to Public University Students, is a division of the Michigan Conference Public Campus Ministries Department. The office of CAMPUS is based in Ann Arbor, Michigan, near the University of Michigan. The following are the core principles that define the CAMPUS approach to ministry: (1) *Vision*: A Bible-based revival movement in which every student is a missionary; (2) *Methodology*: Biblical simplicity; (3) *Philosophy*: Academic excellence and spiritual excellence; (4) *Goal*: Double our membership every year; (5) *Watchword*: Each one reach one; (6) *Mission*: To prepare secular university campuses for the imminent return of Christ; (7) *Motto*: Taking Higher Education Higher. For more information, see www.campushope.com.

72 As mentioned in footnote 3 of the Introduction, CAMPUS runs a Missionary Training Program in Ann Arbor, Michigan, near the University of Michigan campus. It is a two-semester, hands-on program that combines sound classroom instruction with practical field training in ministry and outreach activities. The classes are taught by dedicated staff and guest instructors. The goal of the Missionary Training Program is to develop godly and effective leaders, brilliant and winsome soul winners, and sound spiritual counselors for college/university campuses and other professional environments. Limited to no more than a dozen serious students at a time, the program duration overlaps with the academic year at the University of Michigan.

73 Among other things, CAMPUS has earned the trust of students and young people as the place where lives are transformed and where brilliant and godly leaders are developed. It is one of the few ministries that have succeeded in actually creating a truly racially diverse and mission-driven student movement. CAMPUS is the birthplace and sponsor of GYC (Generation of Youth for Christ)—a thriving, grass-roots revival movement organized and led by young adults (www.gycweb.org). Besides GYC, CAMPUS has also spawned movements with such acronyms as ALIVE, ANEW, l.e.a.d.s., STRIDE, Advent/Campus HOPE, ExCEL, L-I-N-K, p.r.e.s.s, and others.

74 The above expressions are from E. G. White's *In Heavenly Places*, p. 54.

75 Young Martin Luther uttered those words when he was called before Emperor Charles V at the Diet of Worms ("diet" meaning a formal meeting, not a weight-loss plan, and Worms being a city south of Frankfurt in Germany). The statement here cited is from J. H. Merle d'Aubigné's *History of the Reformation of the Sixteenth Century*, book 7, chapter 8, as quoted in E .G. White's *The Great Controversy*, p. 156 (bold emphasis mine).

76 E. G. White, *The Great Controversy*, p. 156; emphasis supplied.

PART 7
THE UN
STORY

The Gre

Betraya

TOLD

ntest

"Truth is not only violated by falsehood; it may be equally outraged by silence."

Henri Frederic Amiel
Swiss Philosopher, Poet, and Critic, 1821–1881

THE TRAVESTY OF JUSTICE

Jesus Christ is arguably the most influential figure in human history. Every year, millions around the world celebrate His birth. Countless others profess to follow His teachings. Movies, such as The Passion of the Christ, have tried to capture the physical horrors of His death. And millions of believers annually remember His resurrection from the dead.

Yet, few are aware that the trials which led to the execution of capital punishment upon Jesus were the greatest travesty of justice.

Like Naboth, whose integrity and tragic murder engaged our attention through much of this book, Christ was also condemned to die for blaspheming "God and King." Hence, Christ's trial proceeded upon a twofold legal path—one process conducted under Hebrew law and the other under Roman law.

Concerning the intersection of these two systems of jurisprudence, the famed British legal scholar and church historian, Alexander Taylor Innes, insightfully wrote two centuries ago:

> "By common consent of lawyers, the most august of all jurisprudences is that of ancient Rome. But perhaps the most peculiar of all jurisprudences, and in the eyes of Christendom the most venerable as well as peculiar, is that of the Jewish Commonwealth. And whenever these two famous and diverse systems happen for a moment to intersect each other, the investigation, from a legal point of view, of the transaction in which they meet is necessarily interesting. But when the two systems meet in the most striking and influential event that has ever happened, its investigation at once becomes not only interesting, but important. It becomes, undoubtedly, the most interesting isolated problem which historical jurisprudence can present."

We cannot, therefore, conclude our study of "Integrity in a Culture of Silence" without reflecting on the judicial trial of Christ. This untold story forms the backdrop for the death and resurrection of Christ—two central events in the life of history's most influential Figure. The trial will also reveal the greatest betrayal of trust in human history—a betrayal prefigured by the principal actors in Naboth's story.

For this final section of Not for Sale, I have selected chapters from Christian author Jerry D. Thomas's Messiah. These chapters expose the violations of religious and civil law following Christ's arrest, through His trial, to His undeserved crucifixion. Based on the book The Desire of Ages, a work judged by millions as the best devotional work on the life of Christ, Messiah captures one of the most moving accounts of the last twenty-four hours of Christ's life.

We are going to look at three major episodes or Acts in the greatest betrayal in history: Act I deals with Christ's trial before Annas and the court of Caiaphas—the two most powerful religious leaders; Act II captures Christ's trial in the judgment hall of Pilate; and Act III portrays the undeserved execution of Christ at Calvary.

ACT I: THE ILLEGAL TRIAL[80]

"If what I said is true, why do you hit me?" (John 18:23)

The guards hurried Jesus through the quiet streets of the sleeping city. It was past midnight. With His hands still tied, the Savior moved painfully to the palace of Annas, a former high priest. Annas was the oldest member of the family in control of the Jewish priests and temple. Because of his age, the people respected him as if he were still the high priest. To many, his advice was like the opinion of God.

Annas had to be in charge when the prisoner was questioned. He was afraid the younger Caiaphas—the actual high priest—might not have the force of will and trickery to push Jesus' death sentence through.

Before Jesus was tried officially in front of the Jewish court—the Sanhedrin—Annas was going to question Him. Under Roman law, the Sanhedrin could make judgments about prisoners, but the Roman authorities had to approve them. So they had to press criminal charges against Jesus that both the Romans and the Jews would accept.

A number of the priests and leaders had been touched by Jesus' teachings. Since everyone knew they supported Jesus, Joseph of Arimathea and Nicodemus were not called to the meeting. But others might insist on a fair trial. Their evidence had to convince the council that Jesus was guilty.

They needed to charge Jesus with two crimes. If they proved that He blasphemed against God (falsely claiming to be God or be as powerful as God), the Jews would condemn Him. If they proved that He was leading a rebellion, the Romans would condemn Him.

Annas tried to prove the second crime first. He questioned Jesus, trying to trick Him into saying something that would prove He was trying to create a secret plan to set up a new kingdom.

But Jesus knew what Annas was trying to do. " 'I have spoken openly to everyone,' " He said. " 'I have always taught in the synagogues and in the Temple, where all the Jews come together. I never said anything in secret' " (John 18:20). It was obvious that Jesus was comparing His way of working to theirs. They had hunted Him down and brought Him to a secret trial, allowing Him to be abused along the way. They broke their own law that said a man was innocent until proven guilty.

Then Jesus turned the question on Annas. "Why are you questioning Me?" The priests' spies had listened to Him every day. "Ask the ones who heard Me teach. They know what I said."

Annas was too angry to speak. But one of his guards hit Jesus in the face. "Is that any way to answer the high priest?" he shouted.

Jesus answered calmly, " 'If I said something wrong, then show what it was. But if what I said is true, why do you hit me?' " (John 18:23) His answer came from a patient, sinless heart that would not be pushed to anger.

Jesus was shamed in every way by those for whom He was making the ultimate sacrifice. His holiness and hate of sin made His suffering worse because being surrounded by people under Satan's control was sickening to Him. And His trial was even harder to bear because He knew that with His divine power, He could destroy His tormentors in a flash.

The Jews were expecting a Messiah who would change people's thoughts and force them to recognize who he was. Jesus was strongly tempted to do just this—to force these priests into admitting that He was their Messiah. It was difficult for Him to set aside His divine power and take their abuse as a human.

The angels of heaven wanted so much to rescue Jesus. As they witnessed the shameful actions of the priests, they were ready to sweep down and destroy them. But they were commanded not to. It was part of Jesus' mission to suffer as a human all the abuse that humans could throw at Him.

On to Caiaphas and the Sanhedrin

Although Jesus stood with His hands tied, showing that He had already been condemned, the Jewish leaders needed to make it look like a legal trial. But they had to do it quickly. They knew how much the people loved Jesus and were afraid that there might be an attempt to rescue Him. If they couldn't force the execution immediately, there would be a week's delay because of Passover. With that much time, thousands of people would come forward to testify about the mighty miracles Jesus had done. The Sanhedrin's actions would be thrown out and Jesus would be freed. Knowing all this, the Jewish leaders were determined to hand Jesus over to the Romans as a criminal who deserved to die before anyone else learned of their plans.

But first, they had to find some crime to charge Jesus with. Annas ordered Jesus to be taken to Caiaphas. With torches and lanterns, the armed guards led their prisoner through the dark early morning hours to the high priest's palace. Although not as forceful as Annas, Caiaphas was just as cruel and deceitful. While the members of the Sanhedrin gathered, Annas and Caiaphas questioned Jesus again. But Jesus said nothing.

When they gathered in the judgment hall of the Sanhedrin, Caiaphas sat on a throne as the presiding officer. On either side of him were judges and leaders. Roman soldiers were stationed on the platform below the throne. At the foot of the throne stood Jesus. In the intense excitement, only Jesus was calm and quiet.

Caiaphas had seen Jesus as his rival, his chief competitor for the attention and respect of the people. And he was bitterly jealous of their eagerness to see and hear Jesus. But now as he looked at the prisoner, Caiaphas admired the noble, dignified way Jesus stood. It struck him that this man was somehow like God. But in the next instant, he banished that thought and demanded that Jesus work one of His mighty miracles. Jesus showed no sign of even hearing his words.

The Jewish leaders were stuck, not sure how to get Jesus condemned. There were plenty of witnesses to prove that Jesus had called the priests hypocrites and murderers, but they didn't want to bring that out. And the Romans wouldn't be interested. There was much evidence that Jesus spoke irreverently about the Jewish ceremonies. But the Romans would see no crime in that either. They didn't dare accuse Jesus of breaking the Sabbath or the stories of His healing miracles would come out.

They called the false witnesses who had been bribed to accuse Jesus of trying to start a rebellion against Rome. But their testimony was weak and with only a few questions they contradicted themselves.

Early in His ministry, Jesus had said, "Destroy this temple and I will build it again in three days." He was talking about His death and resurrection. But of all the things Jesus had said, these were the only words they could find to use against Him. The Romans had rebuilt the temple and took great pride in it. They would not like to hear someone talking about destroying it. On this, the Jews and Romans agreed.

One bribed witness declared, "I heard this man say 'I can destroy God's temple and rebuild it in three days.'" If Jesus' words had been reported exactly as He said them, the Sanhedrin wouldn't have found them strong enough to convict Him. But even as much as the witness had twisted them, Jesus' words weren't a crime worthy of death in the Romans' eyes.

By now, Jesus' accusers were confused, enraged, and desperate. Their last chance was that Jesus would somehow condemn Himself. Caiaphas leaned down from the judgment throne and demanded, "Aren't you going to answer any of these charges against you?" But Jesus said nothing.

Finally Caiaphas asked in a solemn oath, "I command you by the power of the living God: Tell us if you are the Messiah, the Son of God."

Jesus knew that to answer this question would be His death sentence. But this was asked in the name of God by the highest authority in the nation. He had taught His disciples to stand up and tell others who He was. Now He repeated the lesson by His example.

Every eye was locked on Jesus' face as He answered. "Those are your words," Jesus said. A heavenly light seemed to illuminate His pale face as He went on. " 'But I tell you, in the future you will see the Son of Man sitting at the right hand of God, the Powerful One, and coming on clouds in the sky' " (Matthew 26:64).

Caiaphas Is Almost Convinced

For a frozen moment in time, Caiaphas trembled before the penetrating eyes of the Savior. For the rest of his life, he never forgot that look from the Son of God.

The thought that everyone would stand before God and be rewarded for their deeds terrified Caiaphas. In his mind, he saw the final Judgment Day with the dead rising to share secrets he hoped were hidden forever. He felt as if the Eternal Judge was reading his soul and the secrets there.

But in an instant, Caiaphas snapped back. He didn't believe in resurrection or a judgment day anyway. Now, with satanic fury, he ripped his robe and demanded that the prisoner be condemned for blasphemy. "This man has said things that are against God! We don't need any more witnesses. How shall we judge him?"

His fellow priests and leaders agreed. "He must die!" they shouted.

Caiaphas was furious with himself for momentarily believing Jesus. Instead of opening his heart and confessing that Jesus was the Messiah, he ripped open his priestly robes. By trying to cover his horror at Jesus' words, Caiaphas had condemned himself and shown that he was not qualified to be a priest.

According to the laws given through Moses, a high priest must never tear his robe. Their service in the sanctuary demanded that their robes be in perfect condition. Later rabbis had created a law that allowed the high priest to rip his robe in horror at sin, but this was never God's law. When Caiaphas ripped his robe, his act symbolized the Jewish nation's rejection of the Messiah. Now Israel was divorced from God.

The Illegal Trial

The Sanhedrin condemned Jesus to die even though it was against Jewish law to try a prisoner at night. Legally, nothing could be done except during daylight before a full meeting of the council. In spite of this, the Savior was now treated like a condemned criminal.

As Jesus was taken to a guardroom, every person along the way mocked Him and His claim to be the Son of God. His own words—"coming on clouds in the sky"—were repeated as a joke to make fun of Him. While He waited there for His legal trial, Jesus was not protected as even a normal criminal might be. The ignorant mob, made up of some of the cruelest, most degraded people in the city, was allowed to abuse Him verbally and physically. Controlled by demons, Jesus' calm, godlike attitude drove them mad. No criminal was ever treated as badly as was the Son of God.

But the deepest pain Jesus felt didn't come from an enemy's hand. While He was being tried before Caiaphas, one of His own disciples had denied knowing Him.

Before the Rooster Crows Twice

Peter and John had followed the mob that arrested Jesus at a distance. When they came to the Sanhedrin hall of judgment, the priests recognized John and let him inside. They hoped that when John witnessed what happened to Jesus, he would stop believing that this could be the Son of God. John asked them to allow Peter in as well, and they did.

A fire was burning in the courtyard outside the hall, and Peter joined the people huddled around it trying to keep warm. By mingling with them, Peter hoped to be mistaken for one of the crowd who had arrested Jesus.

But the woman who watched the door saw the sadness in Peter's face and asked, "Aren't you one of his disciples?" Peter was startled and confused. He pretended not to understand her. But she kept asking.

Finally, Peter had to answer. "I don't know him," he said. At that moment, a rooster crowed. A short time later, someone else accused him of being a follower of Jesus. This time Peter swore, "I do not know the man!"

An hour later, a relative of the man whose ear Peter had cut off confronted him. "Didn't I see you in the Garden with him? You must be one of them—you're obviously from Galilee."

Trying to deceive them, Peter acted angry, cursing and swearing that he didn't know Jesus at all. As the words left his mouth, the rooster crowed again. Suddenly, Peter remembered Jesus' words: "Before the rooster crows twice, you will say three times that you don't know Me."

With the curses still on his lips and the sound of the rooster still in his ears, Peter's eyes were drawn to where Jesus stood in the hall. At that moment, Jesus turned and looked at Peter—not with anger, but with pity and deep sadness.

The sadness on Jesus' face pierced Peter's heart like an arrow. He remembered his promise given only a few hours before. Now he realized how well Jesus had read his heart and seen the weakness there. A tide of memories washed over him—memories of Jesus' love and patience and his own lies and pride. As he stared, another evil hand rose up and struck his Master in the face again. Heartbroken, unable to watch for even another second, Peter rushed out of the courtyard in the darkness.

Peter ran without thinking or caring until he found himself back in Gethsemane. He replayed his bitter memories of Jesus suffering alone, of not being able to stay awake and pray, of ignoring Jesus' appeal that he pray to avoid falling into sin. It tortured him to know that he had given Jesus the most pain that night. Peter fell to the ground and wished that he could die.

If those hours in the Garden had been spent in prayer, Peter wouldn't have been depending on his own strength—he wouldn't have denied knowing Jesus. If the disciples had witnessed Jesus' agony in the Garden, they would have been prepared for His suffering on the cross. They would have had hope in the dark hours ahead.

Condemning Jesus One More Time

As soon as it was daylight, the Sanhedrin met again and Jesus was brought back before them. They couldn't condemn Him immediately, because many of those now present had not heard His words at the night meeting. And they knew the Roman authorities would not consider Jesus' words worthy of a death sentence. But if they could get Jesus to claim to be the Messiah, they might be able to twist His words to sound like a plan to lead a rebellion.

"If you are the Messiah, tell us," they demanded. But Jesus said nothing. They kept badgering Him until He finally said, "If I tell you, you will not believe Me. And if I ask you, you will not answer." Then He added a solemn warning. " 'But from now on, the Son of Man will sit at the right hand of the powerful God' " (Luke 22:69).

This was the opening they had hoped for. "Then are you the Son of God?" they asked.

Jesus answered, "You say that I am."

This was all they needed. They cried out, "Why do we need any other witnesses? We heard him say it himself." So once again, Jesus was condemned to die. All they needed now was for the Roman authority to agree.

Once again, this time in the presence of the Jewish priests and leaders, Jesus was beaten and abused. When the judges announced the death sentence, a satanic fury took possession of the people watching and they rushed toward Jesus. If armed Roman soldiers hadn't stepped in, Jesus would not have lived to be nailed to the cross—He would have been torn to pieces.

These Roman officers—even though they knew nothing about God—were angry at the brutal treatment of someone who had not been proven guilty of anything. They pointed out that it was against Jewish law to condemn a man to death based on his own testimony. But the Jewish leaders had no shame or pity.

Priests and leaders forgot the dignity of their offices as they shouted curses at the Son of God. They taunted Jesus about His mother being pregnant before she was married. They said that claiming to be the Messiah meant that He should die in the most horrible way. An old coat was thrown over His head and people struck Him in the face, shouting, "Prove that you are a prophet, you Messiah. Tell us who hit you!"

Angels recorded every blow, every word, every look of these evil men against their beloved Commander. One day the same men who shouted in, spit at, and struck the face of Jesus will see it shining with glory brighter than the sun.

ACT 2: THE ROMAN TRIAL[81]

"This is why I was born and came into the world: to tell people the truth."
(John 18:37)

Jesus stood—tied like a prisoner, surrounded by guards—in the judgment hall of Pilate, the Roman governor. The hall was filling with spectators. Just outside were the priests, others of the Sanhedrin, and the mob.

After condemning Jesus, the Sanhedrin came to Pilate to have the death sentence confirmed and carried out. But these Jewish leaders would not enter the hall. According to their ceremonial laws, entering would have made them unclean and forced them to miss Passover. They couldn't see that their hate had already made them unclean or that since they had rejected the true Passover Lamb, the festival no longer had any purpose.

Pilate was not feeling friendly. He had been called from his bed and was determined to get his work done quickly and return to it. Putting on his most stern expression, he turned to see what kind of man he had to question.

Pilate had dealt with many criminals, but never had someone who seemed so noble and good been brought to him. He saw no sign of guilt or fear or angry defiance on Jesus' face. He saw a man whose face showed the mark of heaven. His wife had told him about the prophet from Galilee who could heal the sick and raise the dead. Remembering rumors he had heard from other sources, Pilate turned to the Jews and asked, "Who is this man and why have you brought him here?"

"He is a liar called Jesus of Nazareth," they answered.

So Pilate asked again, "What charges do you have against this man?"

The priests were offended that he would question their decision. They said, " 'If he were not a criminal, we wouldn't have brought him to you' "(John 18:30). They hoped that Pilate would give them what they wanted without any delay.

Pilate had quickly condemned innocent men before. In his mind, a prisoner's guilt or innocence was not really important—he did whatever was politically helpful. The priests hoped that Pilate would pass the death sentence on Jesus without even a hearing.

But something about Jesus held Pilate back. He remembered that Jesus had raised Lazarus from the grave after four days. He wanted to know what crimes Jesus was charged with before he would agree to have Him killed. "If your decision is all that is needed, why bring him to me? Judge him by your own laws," Pilate told them.

They explained that they had judged Him and sentenced Him to death. But they needed Pilate to enforce the sentence. As morally weak as he was, this time Pilate refused to condemn Jesus until he heard some criminal charge against Him.

The priests were trapped. They couldn't allow it to seem that Jesus had been arrested on religious charges, because Pilate wouldn't care about that. What really worried the Romans were signs of a rebellion against them. So they called false witnesses to say, "We caught this man misleading the people, telling them not to pay taxes to Rome, and calling himself the Messiah, a king." They had no evidence for any of these charges, but the priests were willing to lie to get what they wanted.

Pilate Recognizes a Plot

Pilate didn't believe that this prisoner schemed against the Roman government. He knew a plot to destroy an innocent man when he heard one. Turning to Jesus, he asked, "Are you the King of the Jews?"

Jesus answered, "Those are your words." As He spoke, His face lit up as if touched by a beam of sunlight.

Hearing Jesus' words, Caiaphas insisted that Pilate himself had heard Jesus admit to the crimes. Pilate turned to Jesus. "Don't you hear them accusing you of these things? What do you say?" But Jesus said nothing. He stood untouched by the waves of anger and abuse that broke around Him.

Pilate was astonished. "Doesn't this man want to save his own life?" he wondered. He couldn't believe that Jesus was as evil as the shouting priests. To escape the roar of the angry crowd, he pulled Jesus off to one side and asked again, "Are you the King of the Jews?"

Jesus could see that the Holy Spirit was working on Pilate's heart and gave him a chance to respond. "Is that your own question, or did others tell you about Me?"

Pilate understood what Jesus was asking, but he wouldn't admit to a personal interest in the Savior. "I am not Jewish," he answered. "Your own people and your leaders and priests handed you over to me. What have you done wrong?"

Jesus still tried to teach Pilate. He said, "My kingdom does not belong to this world. If it did, My servants would fight to free Me from the Jews. But My kingdom is from another place."

Pilate nodded. "So you are a king!"

Jesus answered, " 'You are the one saying I am a king. This is why I was born and came into the world: to tell people the truth. And everyone who belongs to the truth listens to me' " (John 18:37). Jesus wanted Pilate to know that only by accepting truth could his twisted character be repaired.

Pilate was confused. In his heart, he longed to know what this truth really was and how he could find it. "What is truth?" he asked. But he didn't wait for an answer. He went back out to where the screaming priests wanted some immediate action and declared, "I find no guilt in this man at all."

When the priests heard this, they nearly went mad with disappointment and rage. Rather than see Jesus released, they seemed ready to tear Him to pieces with their own hands. They shouted criticisms of Pilate, threatening to report him to Rome since he refused to condemn a man who claimed to be king instead of Caesar. Angry voices declared, "He stirs up people to rebel across the land, from Galilee to here."

At this point, Pilate didn't even consider condemning Jesus. He knew that the Jews accused Jesus because of their hate and jealousy. The right thing to do would be to release Jesus. But Pilate knew that if he did, the Jews would create problems for him. When he heard that Jesus was from Galilee, he decided to send Him to Herod who was king of that province. This would put the responsibility for what happened on Herod and maybe end an old quarrel between them.

Trial at Herod's Palace

Followed by the jeering mob, Jesus was rushed through the streets of Jerusalem to the palace where Herod was staying. Herod, the same king who had put John the Baptist to death, was delighted to see Jesus because he had heard so much about Him and wanted to see one of His miracles. When Herod first heard about Jesus, he had been afraid that it was John the Baptist come back to life. But now he had the chance to save the life of a prophet and silence the memory of John's death. Herod was sure that Jesus would do whatever he asked in order to be released.

When the Savior was brought in, the priests quickly began explaining their charges against Him. But Herod commanded them to be silent. He ordered Jesus to be untied and accused the Jews of mistreating the prisoner. He was as quickly convinced as Pilate that Jesus was being falsely accused. Herod began to ask Jesus questions, but Jesus kept silent. At the king's command, sick and lame people were brought in and Jesus was commanded to prove who He was by healing them. Jesus did not respond. Herod kept urging, "Show us that you have the power we've heard about."

But the Son of God had taken human nature and He would only do what any human could have done under those circumstances. He would not perform a miracle to save Himself from pain and humiliation.

Herod promised that if Jesus would perform a miracle, He would be released. The Jewish leaders were terrified that Jesus would do it—certainly they knew that He could. If He did, their plans would be ruined and likely they themselves would be killed. They began to shout, "He is a traitor and a blasphemer! He works his miracles by the power of the devil!"

Herod's conscience had been dulled since the days when he trembled at Herodias's request for John the Baptist's head. His loose lifestyle had degraded his morals so badly that he even boasted about killing John. Now he threatened to have Jesus killed if He didn't respond. But Jesus gave no indication that He even heard the words.

Jesus' silence irritated Herod. He seemed to have no respect for Herod's authority. Once again, Herod threatened Jesus with death, but again Jesus was silent.

Jesus' mission did not include amusing the curious. If His words would have healed souls sick from sin, He would have spoken. But He had no words for someone who trampled truth as Herod had done with John the Baptist. Herod had rejected John's words and he would be given no more messages. Jesus had no words for this arrogant king who felt no need of a Savior.

So angry that his face was red, Herod declared that Jesus was an imposter. "If you won't prove who you claim to be, I will hand you over to the soldiers and the mob. If you are an imposter, you deserve to die. If you are the Son of God, save yourself by working a miracle."

At that instant, the crowd leaped at Jesus like wild animals attacking their prey. Jesus was dragged back and forth as Herod joined in to try to humiliate the Son of God. Once again, if the Roman soldiers hadn't stepped in, Jesus would have been torn to pieces. Then Herod had his soldiers wrap a kingly robe around Jesus' shoulders and they joined the Jewish leaders in the worst abuse they could manage. But Jesus still said nothing.

A few people who came up to mock Jesus turned back, silent and afraid. Even Herod had to step back, suddenly concerned. The last rays of mercy were shining into his sin-hardened heart. Divinity flashed through the human form of Jesus and Herod felt like he was seeing God on His throne. As calloused as he was, he suddenly didn't dare send Jesus to His death. Instead Herod sent Him back to the Roman judgment hall.

The Last Trial Before Pilate

Pilate was disappointed to find the Jews bringing Jesus back. He reminded them that he had already found Jesus innocent. And Herod, a king of their own country, had not agreed to sentence Him. "I will punish him and let him go free," he announced.

But this showed Pilate's weakness. Jesus was innocent, but he was willing to have Him whipped to try to please the Jewish leaders. If Pilate had stood firm, refusing to condemn a man who was innocent, he would have escaped the chains of regret that haunted the rest of his life. Jesus would have been killed anyway, but Pilate would not have held any guilt for it. But Pilate, having ignored his conscience so many times before, was almost helpless in the face of the pressure from the priests and leaders.

But Pilate was still given help from heaven. An angel had given his wife a dream where she spoke with Jesus. Pilate's wife was not a Jew, but seeing Jesus in her dream, she knew He was the Son of God. She saw Pilate have Jesus whipped, then declare, "I find Him innocent." She saw him give Jesus to His murderers. She saw the cross, the strange darkness, and heard the mysterious cry, "It is finished." Then she saw Jesus seated on a white cloud and His murderers trying to escape His glory. With a cry of horror, she woke up and immediately wrote a message to Pilate.

The note rushed to him by messenger said, "Don't do anything to that innocent Man. Today I had a very troubling dream about Him."

Pilate's face paled. He was confused by his own conflicting emotions. And while he delayed, the priests were stirring up the anger of the crowd. Then he remembered a custom the Jews cherished that he might use to free Jesus. At Passover time, the Jewish people were often allowed to choose one prisoner to be released from jail. The Romans were holding a prisoner named Barabbas who was already sentenced to die. Barabbas pretended to be a religious revolutionary who was trying to overthrow the Romans. But in reality, he was just a common criminal trying to get rich by robbing others.

By giving the people a choice between this thief and the clearly innocent Jesus, Pilate was appealing to their sense of justice. He shouted out his question. "Who do you want me to set free? Barabbas or Jesus, who is called the Messiah?"

The answer was like the bellow of a wild animal. "Give us Barabbas!"

Thinking that they couldn't have understood his question, Pilate asked again, "Do you want me to free the King of the Jews?"

The crowd roared even louder. "Take this man away and set Barabbas free!"

Pilate cried out, "Then what should I do with Jesus the Messiah?"

Demons in human form stood in the crowd and led out in the answering shout: "Crucify him!"

Pilate never thought it would come to that. He cringed at the thought of sending an innocent man to that most cruel death. "Why? What has he done wrong?" he asked. But it was too late for a logical argument. Pilate tried once more to save Jesus. He asked again, "What has he done wrong?"

But this only stirred the mob up more. They cried out louder and louder. "Crucify him! Crucify him!"

Pilate finally commanded that Jesus be beaten with whips. Already weak and covered with cuts and bruises, Jesus was whipped and led into a room where the soldiers gathered. They shaped a crown out of thorny branches and put it on Jesus' head. Then they wrapped a purple robe around Him and mocked Him. "Hail the King of the Jews!" they called out as they struck Him in the face and spit on Him. Often someone struck the crown, forcing the thorns into His scalp and sending blood trickling down His face.

An enraged mob surrounded the Savior of the world. Mocking and jeering laughs were mixed with cursing and blasphemy. Satan himself led this mob. His plan was to provoke Jesus into striking back or performing a miracle to save Himself. Just one sin, one slip-up, and the plan to save humans would have failed. But Jesus endured it all, peacefully and calmly.

Jesus' enemies had demanded a miracle to prove His divinity. This was the greatest evidence they could have asked for. His patience and humility in these circumstances proved His relationship with God. Satan was greatly angry when he saw that Jesus remained faithful to His Father's will.

When Pilate sent Jesus to be beaten, he hoped that this punishment would satisfy the crowd. But the Jews saw the weakness of claiming someone was innocent and then punishing them anyway. They pressed even harder, determined to see Jesus die.

Pilate had Barabbas brought to the court to stand side-by-side with Jesus. Pointing to the Savior, he said, "Look at this man!" There stood the Son of God, stripped to the waist, blood flowing freely from the long gashes in His back. His face was strained and bruised, but never more beautiful. Every feature on His face communicated tender pity for His enemies. He showed strength and dignity in spite of His pain.

The prisoner beside Him seemed the very opposite. Every line on Barabbas's face said that he was a tough thug. The difference between them was clear to everyone. Some in the crowd wept with sympathy as they looked at Jesus. Even the priests and leaders were persuaded that Jesus was all He claimed to be.

The Roman soldiers who surrounded Jesus were not all hard-hearted. As they watched Jesus with pity, His silent surrender was stamped in their hearts. This scene never faded from their minds until they decided to follow this Savior or reject Him forever.

Pilate was sure that the sight of Jesus next to Barabbas would find sympathy with the Jews. But he didn't understand the fanatical hate of the priests. Once again, the priests and leaders led the crowd in that awful chant: "Crucify him! Crucify him!"

Finally, Pilate lost his patience with their unreasonable cruelty and cried out sadly, "Take him then, and crucify him. I find nothing against him."

The priests answered, "We have a law that says he should die, because he claimed to be the Son of God."

This startled Pilate. He hadn't known that this might be a divine being standing before him. He turned back to Jesus and asked, "Where are you from?" But Jesus didn't answer. He had spoken to Pilate before and explained His mission. Pilate had ignored the truth. He had abused the power of his office by caving in to the demands of the mob. Jesus had nothing else to say.

Annoyed at Jesus' silence, Pilate spoke arrogantly. "You refuse to speak to me? Don't you know I have the power to set you free or to have you crucified?"

This Jesus answered. " 'The only power you have over me is the power given to you by God. The man who turned me in to you is guilty of a greater sin' " (John 19:11). Jesus was talking about Caiaphas who represented the Jewish nation. They had the prophecies of the Messiah and the unmistakable evidence of Jesus' divinity. The leaders had the greatest responsibility for what the Jews did to Jesus. Pilate, Herod, and the Roman soldiers were mostly ignorant about Jesus. If they had had the light the Jews had, the soldiers would not have treated Jesus like they did.

Once again, Pilate suggested letting Jesus go free. But the Jews cried out, "If you let this man go, you are no friend of Caesar's." No country hated the domination of the Roman power more than the Jews. But to get rid of Jesus, the Jewish leaders would swear loyalty to the foreign power they hated. "Anyone who makes himself a king is against Caesar," they added.

Pilate was already under suspicion from Rome. A report that he was allowing people to call themselves king would ruin him. And he knew the Jews would stop at nothing for revenge if he stopped their plans. But Pilate presented Jesus to the crowd one more time, saying, "Here is your king!"

And again the mad cry rang out: "Take him away! Crucify him!"

In a voice that rang through the courtyard, Pilate asked, "Do you want me to crucify your king?"

From the unholy lips of the crowd came the answer: "The only king we have is Caesar!" By choosing a heathen king, the Jews rejected God as their King. From then on, Caesar was their king. The priests and rabbis had led the people to this and they were responsible for the terrible things that would soon follow.

When Pilate saw that he could do nothing and that a riot was starting, he called for a basin of water and washed his hands in front of them all. Then he said, "I am not guilty of this man's death. You are responsible for it."

Pilate looked at Jesus, sure in his heart that He was a God. Turning again to the crowd, he said, "I am innocent of His blood. Crucify Him if you must, but I declare that He is innocent. May the One He claims is His Father judge you and not me for this." Then he said to Jesus, "Forgive me for this. I cannot save You." Then he had Jesus beaten with whips once more and sent Him to be crucified.

Pilate wanted to save Jesus, but he couldn't do it and save his own position. He chose to sacrifice an innocent Person rather than lose his power. Many today sacrifice their principles for the same reasons. Our conscience and duty point one way while our looking out for ourselves point in another.

In spite of his efforts, the very thing Pilate feared happened. He was soon thrown out of office. Hurt by regrets and wounded pride, not long after the Crucifixion, Pilate ended his own life.

When Pilate declared that he was innocent of Jesus' blood, Caiaphas answered defiantly, "We and our children will be responsible for his death." Those awful words were echoed by the people. The whole crowd roared, "We and our children will be responsible for his death."

The people of Israel chose Barabbas, the murderer and thief, and rejected their Messiah. In making this choice, they accepted Satan as their leader. Now they would live under his rules. When they cried, "We and our children will be responsible for his death," their prayer was heard. They were responsible for the destruction of Jerusalem in a few short years and for the fate of the Jewish nation for the next two thousand years.

And that prayer will be answered again on the great Judgment Day. Jesus will return in glory with thousands of angels as an escort. In the place of thorns, He will wear a crown of glory. On His robe will be the words, "King of kings and Lord of lords."

The same priests and leaders will see again the scenes in those judgment halls. Every thing that happened will be written out in letters of fire. Then those who prayed, "We and our children will be responsible for his death" will see what they asked for. In their shame and horror, they will beg the rocks and mountains to fall on them.

ACT 3:[82] THE EXECUTION[83]

"Jesus cried out, 'Father, I give you my life'" (Luke 23:46)

The news that Jesus had been condemned to die spread quickly and people of all types flocked toward the place where crucifixions were done. The priests held to their agreement not to harass Jesus' disciples if Jesus was given to them, so many disciples and followers of Jesus joined the crowds.

Three crosses had been prepared for Barabbas and two of his thieves who were scheduled to die that day. The cross that had been ready for Barabbas was placed on Jesus' bleeding shoulders. Since the Passover supper, Jesus had had nothing to eat or drink. He had suffered the pain of being betrayed and abandoned. He had been rushed from Annas to Caiaphas to Pilate to Herod and back to Pilate. The night had been filled with events that would test the heart of any human. Jesus hadn't failed. He had taken it all with dignity. But after the second beating with the whip, when the cross was laid on His shoulder, His human body could take no more. Jesus collapsed.

The crowd showed no mercy, taunting Jesus because He couldn't carry the cross. The soldiers lifted the cross up and placed it on Him again. Again Jesus fell to the ground. When it was clear that Jesus could not carry the cross, they began to search for someone who could. No Jew would carry it because this would make them unclean for Passover.

Then Simon, a stranger from Cyrene, met the crowd as he came into the city. Simon, astonished at what he saw, expressed pity for the poor Man. So the soldiers grabbed him and forced him to carry the cross for Jesus. Now Simon's sons were followers of Jesus, but Simon was not. Carrying the cross to Calvary turned out to be a real blessing for Simon, because he became a believer in the Messiah that day.

Many women were in the crowd that followed the Savior. Some had brought their sick loved ones to Him to be healed—others had been healed themselves. They were shocked at how the crowd hated Jesus. When Jesus fell under the cross, these women ignored the angry priests and began wailing with sorrow.

Even in His pain and exhaustion, Jesus noticed. He knew that they didn't understand who He was or His sacrifice for them, but He appreciated their sympathy. He said, " 'Women of Jerusalem, don't cry for me. Cry for yourselves and for your children' " (Luke 23:28). He saw forward to the time when Jerusalem would be destroyed and some of these same women would die along with their children.

In the destruction of Jerusalem Jesus saw a symbol of the end of the world. He said, " 'Then people will say to the mountains, "Fall on us!" And they will say to the hills, "Cover us!"

If they act like this now when life good, what will happen when bad times come?' "
(Luke 23:30, 31). God's anger against sin was now focused on His Son. What would the
suffering be like at the end for someone who refused to give up sin?

In the crowd that followed Jesus to Calvary were many who had shouted the hosannas and
waved palm branches when He rode into Jerusalem. More than a few who had shouted
praises that day because everyone else was, now joined in screaming, "Crucify him!" When
Jesus rode into Jerusalem, His disciples pressed close around Him and felt the honor. Now
they followed Him at a distance to escape the humiliation.

Jesus' Mother
When they reached the place of execution, the two thieves fought those who forced them
onto their crosses. Jesus did not resist. Mary, His mother, supported by John, had followed her
Son's steps to Calvary. She wanted so much to put her hand under His head and comfort Him
but this was not permitted. She still held on to the hope that Jesus would save Himself. But in
her heart she remembered that He had predicted these events.

As the thieves were nailed to their crosses, Mary held her breath. Would the One who
could bring the dead to life allow Himself to be crucified? Must she give up her faith that
He was the Messiah? She saw His hands stretched out on the rough wood and the hammer
raised up. When the spikes were driven through His tender flesh, Mary fainted. The disciples
carried her away.

The Savior Is Sacrificed
Jesus did not cry out, but great drops of sweat formed on His forehead. No caring hands
wiped His face, no words of comfort or sympathy were spoken to sooth His human heart.
While the soldiers went about their dreadful work, Jesus prayed, "Father, forgive them, because they don't know what they are doing."

Jesus didn't call down curses on these soldiers who handled Him so roughly. He didn't call
for revenge on the priests and leaders. He only breathed a prayer for their forgiveness because
they didn't understand what they were doing. But this ignorance didn't take away their guilt.
They could have learned about Jesus and accepted Him as their Savior. Some of them would
see their sins, repent, and change. Others would make it impossible for Jesus' prayer to be
answered by not ever repenting. But God's plan was being completed—Jesus was earning the
right to represent all humans to His Father.

Jesus' prayer for His enemies includes every sinner from the beginning of the world to the
end of time. All of us are guilty of crucifying the Son of God. But all are offered forgiveness.

As soon as Jesus was nailed to the cross, it was lifted up by strong men and shoved into its hole
in the rock—causing intense pain for Jesus. Then Pilate had a board inscribed with the words

"Jesus of Nazareth, King of the Jews" nailed to the cross above Jesus' head.

This irritated the Jews, but they were the ones who had claimed Caesar as their true king. The sign declared that whoever else claimed to be king in Israel would be killed. In order to have Jesus killed, the priests had sacrificed their national identity. But they asked Pilate to change the words to "This man said, 'I am the King of the Jews.'"

But Pilate, already angry with himself, replied coldly, "What I have written, I have written."

But God guided the hand that wrote the inscription. People from many lands were in Jerusalem and that sign declaring that Jesus was the Messiah King was noticed. Many people went back to the Scriptures to study the prophecies.

Many prophecies were fulfilled as Jesus suffered on the cross. From the Psalms came predictions that the Messiah's hands and feet would be pierced, and that others would gamble for His clothes. The soldiers at the Crucifixion were given the prisoners' clothes to destroy or keep. Since Jesus' coat was of high quality, the soldiers gambled to decide which of them would keep it.

Another prediction from Psalms said that the suffering Messiah would be offered vinegar to drink. Those who suffered death on the cross were allowed to have an intoxicating drink based on vinegar. But when Jesus tasted it, He refused to drink it. He needed a clear mind to keep focused on God, His only strength. Clouding His senses would only give Satan an advantage.

The Jewish priests and leaders joined the mob in mocking the dying Savior. "If you are the Son of God, come down from there," they shouted. "If he is the Messiah, let him save himself." Satan and his angels—in human form—were there encouraging the priests and stirring up the mob.

The Father's voice from heaven was silent and no one else spoke up for Jesus. He suffered alone. He heard the priests declare, "If he really is the Messiah, let him come down from the cross. Then we will believe in him." Jesus could have come down from the cross. But because He didn't save Himself, sinners have the hope of forgiveness.

One Thief Believes

Jesus felt one gleam of comfort on the cross—the prayer of the repentant thief. Both of the men crucified with Jesus had mocked Him at first and one only became more desperate and defiant as he suffered. But the other was not a hardened criminal. He was less guilty than many who stood beside the cross cursing the Savior. He had seen Jesus and heard Him teach, but had been convinced by the priests not to listen. Trying to quiet his conscience, he plunged into a criminal life until he was arrested and condemned.

On the cross he saw the religious teachers ridicule Jesus. He heard his fellow thief shout, "If you are the Messiah, save yourself and us." Among the crowd he heard many repeating stories of what Jesus had done and said. Once again, he felt sure that this was the Messiah. He turned to the other thief and said, "You should fear God! You are getting the same punishment He is." The thief was beyond fearing humans, but he was now afraid that God no longer cared for him and would judge him harshly. "We are getting what we deserve, but this Man has done nothing wrong."

When he was condemned for his crime, the thief had given up all hope. But now strange, gentle thoughts were stirring in his mind. The Holy Spirit led his thinking step by step until it all made sense to him. In spite of being mocked and hanging on a cross, he saw Jesus as the Lamb of God. Hope mingled with the pain in his voice as he said, "Lord, remember me when You come into Your kingdom."

Quickly the answer came in a voice full of love and power: "Today I tell you the truth—you will be with Me in paradise."

Jesus had listened with a longing heart for some words of faith from His disciples. Instead He had only heard sad doubts: "We believed that He was the One who would save Israel." The dying thief's words of faith encouraged Jesus when no one else would even acknowledge Him.

Those words of faith also got the attention of bystanders. The soldiers gambling over Jesus' clothes stopped to listen. As Jesus spoke His promise, a ray of living light pierced the dark cloud that seemed to cover the cross. Jesus, on the shameful cross, was bathed in glory. Heaven recognized Him as the Bearer of sin. Humans could strip Him of His clothing, but they could not take His power to forgive sins and save all who came to God through Him.

Jesus did not promise that the thief would be with Him in paradise that same day. He Himself did not go to heaven that day. On the morning of the Resurrection, He said, "I have not yet gone up to My Father." But the promise was given "today"—right then as He hung dying on the cross—and the forgiven thief will be with Jesus in heaven.

Jesus was placed in the middle between the two thieves at the request of the priests to show that He was the worst of the criminals. But in the same way, His cross was placed in the middle of a dying world trapped in sin. And His words of forgiveness to the thief are a light that shines hope to the farthest parts of the world. During His suffering, Jesus spoke as a prophet to the women of Jerusalem. As a priest or representative, He asked His Father to forgive His murderers. As the Savior, He forgave the sins of a repented thief.

Mary returned to the foot of the cross, supported by John. She couldn't bear to be away from her Son and John, knowing that the end was near, brought her back. Looking into her grief-filled eyes, Jesus said, "Dear woman, here is your son." Then He said to John, "Here is your mother."

John understood and accepted the responsibility. From that moment he cared for Mary in his own home. Jesus had no money to leave for His mother's care, but He gave her what she needed most—a friend who loved her because she loved Jesus. And John was greatly blessed as well—she was a constant reminder of his beloved Master. Those who follow Jesus will never leave their parents without care or respect.

The Death of Jesus

Now the Lord of glory was near death, deep in depression and agony. It wasn't the fear of death or the pain of the cross that caused His suffering. It was a sense of the horrible wickedness of sin. Jesus saw how few humans would be willing to break their addiction to it. Without help from God, all humans would be exterminated.

The guilt of every human since Adam was placed on Jesus—our Replacement—and it pressed heavily on His heart. All of His life, Jesus had been sharing the good news of the Father's forgiving love. But now with this terrible weight of sin, He could not see the Father's face. This tore at His heart in a way that humans will never fully understand. This agony was so overwhelming that He hardly felt the physical pain.

Satan pressed Jesus' heart with fierce temptations. He did not feel the hope that He would rise from the grave or the hope that the Father would accept Him. Jesus felt the anguish a sinner will feel when no One pleads for mercy for the guilty. It was this sense of sin—the sense that the Father's anger was focused on Him as the Replacement for sinful humans—that broke His heart.

The sun refused to look down on this awful scene. Its bright rays had been lighting the earth at noon when suddenly it seemed to be blotted out. The whole land was dark until three o'clock in the afternoon. This unnatural darkness was as deep as midnight without moon or stars. It was a miraculous sign given by God to strengthen our faith.

God and the holy angels were there beside the cross, hidden in the thick darkness. The Father was with His Son. But His presence had to be hidden. In that terrible hour, Jesus could not be comforted by His Father's presence.

God created the darkness to cover the last human suffering of His Son. All who had seen Jesus suffer that day had been convicted of His divinity. His long hours of torture had been accompanied by the stares and jeers of the mob. Now, mercifully, God hid Him.

When the darkness came, an unexplainable terror came over the crowd gathered around the cross. The cursing and shouting stopped. Brilliant lightning occasionally flashed through the clouds and revealed the crucified Savior. Priests, leaders, soldiers, and the mob thought their payback was coming. Some whispered that Jesus would now come down from the cross.

At three o'clock the darkness lifted from the crowd but still covered Jesus. No one could see through the gloom that shrouded His suffering soul. But Jesus' voice was heard crying, "'My God, my God, why have you rejected me?' " (Matthew 27:46).

Many voices suggested that Jesus was being punished for claiming to be God. Many of His followers who heard His despairing cry gave up all hope. If God had rejected Jesus, what could His followers believe in?

Then the darkness lifted and Jesus revived enough to feel the physical pain. He said, "I am thirsty." One of the Roman soldiers felt pity and offered Jesus a sponge soaked in vinegar. But the priests mocked Jesus again. They misinterpreted Jesus' cry to mean that He was calling for the prophet Elijah and refused to allow Him to have water. "No," they said, "we want to see if Elijah will come and save him."

He Did It for You

The perfect Son of God hung on the cross, His skin slashed by whips. His hands that had so often reached out to bless others were nailed to the wooden planks. His feet, so tireless on missions of love, were spiked to the beam. His royal head was pierced by the crown of thorns; His trembling lips twisted in a cry of pain.

And all that He suffered—the blood that dripped from His head, His hands, and His feet, the agony that tore His body with every breath, and the unspeakable anguish in His heart from being separated from His Father—speaks to each of us, saying, "For you the Son of God agrees to carry this guilt; for you He battles death and wins; for you He opens the gates of heaven; for you He offers Himself as a sacrifice. All of this He does because of His love for you."

Jesus Dies Triumphantly

Suddenly the darkness lifted from the cross. In a voice that seemed to ring through all creation like a trumpet, Jesus cried, "It is finished. Father, I give You My life." A light surrounded the cross and the Savior's face shone like the glory of the sun. Then He hung His head and died.

In the darkness, Jesus drank the cup of human suffering and sin. During those dreadful hours, He fell back on what He had known all His life. By faith, He rested in His Father's love even though He could no longer feel it. And as He surrendered His life to God, the sense of having lost His Father's love vanished. By faith, Jesus won the battle.

Now darkness covered the land again and there was a violent earthquake. In the surrounding mountains, rocks split into pieces and crashed to the plains below. Graves were ripped open and the dead were thrown out. Priests, soldiers, and the others in the crowd fell to the ground in fear.

The moment Jesus cried, "It is finished," was the time of the evening sacrifice at the temple. The lamb that represented the Messiah had been brought in to be killed. The priest stood with the knife in his hand as the people watched. Then the ground trembled, because God Himself was approaching. With a loud ripping sound, the inner curtain of the temple was torn from top to bottom. People stared right into the place that was once filled with the presence of God. The Most Holy Place of the temple was no longer sacred.

There was terror and confusion everywhere. The knife fell from the priest's suddenly numb hand and the lamb escaped. The symbolic intersected with reality. The great sacrifice had been made. A new, living path to salvation was available to everyone. Jesus would now become our Priest, our Representative in heaven.

"Christ was treated as we deserve, that we might be treated as He deserves. He was condemned for our sins, in which He had no share, that we might be justified by His righteousness, in which we had no share. He suffered the death which was ours, that we might receive the life which was His. 'With His stripes we are healed.'"[84]

The Wondrous Cross

At Calvary, Christ displayed the spirit of patient silence. His patience prevailed, even under the excruciating pain of betrayal, malice, injustice, torture, and death. Our Savior calmly endured the suffering because, throughout His life, He had developed the stamina of patience in the school of trials and afflictions (cf. Hebrews 5:8).

All those who choose to follow the Savior in a life of integrity must possess such endurance— patience in the midst of trials and afflictions. "It was to that God called you, for Christ himself suffered for you and left you an example, so that you would follow in his steps. He committed no sin, and no one ever heard a lie come from his lips. When he was insulted, he did not answer back with an insult; when he suffered, he did not threaten, but placed his hopes in God, the righteous Judge."

When, in the face of injustice we are tempted to feel that nobody knows nor understands our sorrow and pain, let us look at the Cross. From the perspective at Calvary, from the shameful crucifixion on the cross, we can gain a better outlook on, and find courage to handle, every episode of injustice, violence, and senseless death.

Therefore, in the words of Isaac Watts, let us also "survey the wondrous cross on which the Prince of Glory died." When we do so, we shall find strength to endure whatever trials the Lord will permit to come our way.

When I survey the wondrous cross
On which the Prince of glory died,
My richest gain I count but loss,
And pour contempt on all my pride.

Forbid it, Lord, that I should boast,
Save in the death of Christ my God!
All the vain things that charm me most,
I sacrifice them to His blood.

See from His head, His hands, His feet,
Sorrow and love flow mingled down!
Did e'er such love and sorrow meet,
Or thorns compose so rich a crown?

His dying crimson, like a robe,
Spreads o'er His body on the tree;
Then I am dead to all the globe,
And all the globe is dead to me.

Were the whole realm of nature mine,
That were a present far too small;
Love so amazing, so divine,
Demands my soul, my life, my all.

[Added by the compilers of Hymns Ancient and Modern]

To Christ, Who won for sinners grace
By bitter grief and anguish sore,
Be praise from all the ransomed race
Forever and forevermore.

NOTES

77 A[lexander] Taylor Innes, *The Trial of Jesus Christ: A Legal Monograph* (Edinburgh: T. & T. Clark, 1899), p. 2. Innes (1833–1912) earned justifiable fame for his brilliance as an advocate and skill as a church historian. His widely acclaimed *The Trial of Jesus Christ*, though extremely rare, can be accessed in digital form on the Internet. A more recent work that looks at the Jewish and Roman illegalities of Christ's trial is Steven W. Allen's *The Illegal Trial of Christ* (Mesa, AZ: Legal Awareness Series, Inc., 2005).

78 Jerry D. Thomas's *Messiah* (Nampa, Idaho: Pacific Press, 2005). The Messiah is a contemporary adaptation of *The Desire of Ages*, the classic work on Jesus life which was penned by E. G. White more than a hundred years ago. Thomas's contemporary adaptation amplifies the beautiful message of this devotional classic, making the sublime themes of the original easier to grasp. First published in 1898, *The Desire of Ages* is available to read online at http://www.whiteestate.org/books/da/da.asp. The selections from *Messiah* are used with the permission of the author, Jerry Thomas, and the publisher, Pacific Press Publishing Association.

79 These three Acts or Episodes are described in chapters 75, 77, and 78 of *The Desire of Ages*.

80 Act I, dealing with Christ's trial before the two most powerful religious leaders in Israel—Annas and Caiaphas—is based on Matthew 26:57-75; 27:1; Mark 14:53-72; 15:1; Luke 22:54-71; and John 18:13-27.

81 Act II—captures Christ's trial in the judgment hall of Pilate. It is based on Matthew 27:2, 11-31; Mark 15:1-20; Luke 23:1-25; John 18:28-40; 19:1-16.

82 Act III—portrays the undeserved execution of Christ at Calvary. It is based on Matthew 27:31-53; Mark 15:20-38; Luke 23:26-46; and John 19:16-30.

83 The original heading in Jerry Thomas's *Messiah* is "Jesus Dies on the Cross.

84 E. G. White, *The Desire of Ages*, 25

85 See my book *Patience in the Midst of Trials and Afflictions* (Ann Arbor: Michigan: Berean Books, 2003).

86 1 Peter 2:21-23, Good News Bible.

PART 8
UNFINIS
STORY

Postscri

HED

ot

"Your silence gives consent."

Plato
Classical Greek Philosopher and Mathematician, 428/427 B.C.–348/347 B.C.

IMPENDING CONFLICT

"Throughout history, it has been the inaction of those who could have acted; the indifference of those who should have known better; the silence of the voice of justice when it mattered most; that has made it possible for evil to triumph."

Haile Selassie
(1892-1975), Emperor of Ethiopia from 1930 to 1974

History paints and repaints the portrait of human nature in the face of crisis. The past offers us inspiration and tells tales of movements, of wars, of atrocities, and of victories. Modern history has seen a rise of collective bravery in standing up for equality, human dignity, and justice, so much so that we doubt that some of the history of human injustice that has been told and retold can be repeated today.

The preceding pages of this book sought to present lessons from the biblical past, so as to shed light on some critical issues in today's church and society—issues upon which the voices of our silence and apathy are louder than the courage of our convictions. Our goal in studying 1 Kings 21 was also to point out possible roles we can choose to play in the climate of the times in which we live.

Naboth lived some 800 years before Christ. He lived in the days of Ahab and Jezebel—a very dark period in Israel's history. When he would not compromise his religious convictions about his vineyard, Naboth was falsely accused of blaspheming "God and the king"—of being an affront to religion and a threat to national security. Fear and religion were then employed to manipulate people to cause Naboth to forfeit his rights and even lose his life. Naboth died for his spiritual integrity, which would not bend to the political marriage between Ahab and Jezebel.

The integrity of Naboth is worthy of emulation, even as his fate reveals the irrationality of religious persecution and the many forms under which it can take shape. Ultimately, the issues surrounding his tragic death had to do with fundamental human rights and freedom of conscience.

Thoughtful students of history and Bible prophecy are aware that similar issues will be at stake whenever and wherever political leaders align themselves with powerful religious forces to enact and enforce religious laws. It has happened before. We witnessed it in the days of Naboth the Jezreelite. It also occured in the days of Christ, especially during the events leading to His betrayal, trial, and crucifixion. And it happened again during the time of the Early Church, through the Middle Ages, and during Reformation times, when millions were martyred for their faith.

It can take place again—in our time.

As we pointed out earlier, there are disturbing signs that, already, a political realignment is taking place in many countries. There are maneuverings in the religious realm and alignments in the political realm. Powerful religious coalitions are working with governments to legislate religious laws. In many lands, the healthy wall of separation between religion and politics, between church and state, is slowly being pulled down. This trend is discernible even in the United States—a nation that has historically maintained "a friendly separation of church state."[87]

Ahab and Jezebel are getting married. Soon Jezebel would use Ahab's seal to persecute conscientious Naboths.

Although God never forces the will or the conscience, Satan's constant resort—to gain control of those whom he cannot otherwise seduce—is compulsion by cruelty. "Through fear or force he endeavors to rule the conscience and to secure homage to himself. To accomplish this, he works through both religious and secular authorities, moving them to the enforcement of human laws in defiance of the law of God."[88]

Unless we learn from history, the days will soon be upon us, when those who honor sound biblical teachings and principles "will be denounced as enemies of law and order, as breaking down the moral restraints of society, causing anarchy and corruption, and calling down the judgments of God upon the earth. Their conscientious scruples will be pronounced obstinacy, stubbornness, and contempt of authority. They will be accused of disaffection toward the government. Ministers who deny the obligation of the divine law will present from the pulpit the duty of yielding obedience to the civil authorities as ordained of God. In legislative halls and courts of justice, commandment keepers will be misrepresented and condemned. A false coloring will be given to their words; the worst construction will be put upon their motives."[89]

As in the case of Naboth's vineyard, the issues that will be at stake in the impending conflict are identity, heritage, and integrity. Biblical truth, the everlasting gospel, and loyalty to God's law will all be bones of contention.[90]

When Ahab and Jezebel get married, the dignitaries of religion and politics, of church and state, will unite to bribe, persuade, or compel all classes to honor falsehood. They will be blind to the fact that the course they adopt will ultimately lead to the persecution of those who conscientiously refuse to do what the majority of the religious and secular world would be requiring them to do. Unfortunately, they will be aided to succeed because of the deafening silence of many good people.

We've explored in the pages of this book—and in the silence and inaction of the "elders and nobles" from the days of Naboth—the reasons people tend to abandon honor and flee from courage. When we know these reasons, we can better monitor our own weaknesses and motivations, so that we will not abandon our principles or allow ourselves to be manipulated into surrendering what we believe to be right.

To bring hope during troubling times, we must be able to exercise our intelligence—to know and to be true protectors of the innocent and real upholders of justice. We must end the recurrence of shameful history and find meaning in the hope offered by truth.

The silent majority are not silent. Their voices of apathy are louder than the courage of their convictions. Cowardly silence, indifference, and neutrality in times of crisis are criminal acts. We must no longer be silent.

Now is the time to stand up and say that the "inheritance of our fathers"—sound biblical teaching, truth, human rights, and freedom of conscience—have been bequeathed to us at too great a price. They are *not for sale!*

NOTES

87 Church historian C. Mervyn Maxwell employs the phrase, "friendly separation of church and state" to describe the uniqueness of the American political experiment. Commenting on the First Amendment of the U.S. Constitution—"Congress shall make no law respecting an establishment of religion, or prohibiting the free exercise thereof"—Maxwell writes: "The grandest achievement of the American Constitution was the creation of a nation with a friendly separation of church and state. The world had never seen such a thing before. Every other nation since ancient times had taxed the people to support a state religion, and most had oppressed religious dissidents. The French Revolution, a little later than the American, experimented with a hostile separation of church and state. Marxist countries have exceeded France's temporary example. But America, with its friendly separation of church and state, salaried no clergy and taxed no congregation. She permitted denominations to proliferate and supported none of them. Her Congress said, 'In God we trust,' but elected not to define whether He is the God of Christians—or of Hindus." See C. Mervyn Maxwell, *God Cares: Volume 2, The Message of Revelation For You and Your Family* (Boise, Idaho: Pacific Press, 1985), p. 343.

88 *The Great Controversy*, p. 590.

89 *Ibid.*

90 The Bible seems to point to this fact in Revelation chapters 12 to 14. For an insightful discussion of this prophecy, see C. Mervyn Maxwell, *God Cares: Volume 2, The Message of Revvelation for You and Your Family*, pp. 309-419. See also Mark Finley, *The Next Superpower: Ancient Prophecies, Global Events, and Your Future* (Hagerstown, MD: Review and Herald, 2005), pp. 109–225. For an insightful discussion of the issues on religious liberty in the light of Bible prophecy, see Christa Reinach and Alan J. Reinach, eds. *Politics and Prophecy: The Battle for Religious Liberty and the Authentic Gospel* (Nampa, Idaho: Pacific Press, 2007).

RECOMMENDED READING

If *Not for Sale*'s message on integrity has been a blessing to you, you will also greatly appreciate some of the other insightful books by the author. These recommended books on patience and love are for all those who seek solid biblical answers and authentic Christian spirituality. (Information about how to obtain them is found at the end of this section.)
Thank You!

AUTHOR'S BOOK ON TRIALS AND AFFLICTIONS

In the journey through life, trials await us all. For at one point or another, every one of us is bound to experience the agony of pain, disappointment, sorrow, hurt, loss, or some other form of suffering that will severely test our resiliency and character. We may also suffer afflictions—prolonged ordeals of suffering that lie deeper in the soul.

God uses these trials and afflictions to cultivate in us the virtue of patience.

You can tell that the Lord is developing patience in you when you run into many anguishing experiences; when the things or people you depend on suddenly fail you; when your life seems to be in detours; when prolonged illness and other forms of affliction plague you; when your situation in life goes from bad to worse. Above all, you know you are being schooled in patience when you cry out to God for help, and He doesn't seem to hear or care.

Patience in the Midst of Trials and Afflictions insightfully explains the nature of patience, why God permits trials and afflictions, and how you can benefit from them. This life-changing book will be a source of encouragement to you and your loved ones. It will give you confidence in God's guidance and renew your determination to trust Him, no matter what.
ISBN: 1-890014-04-4. Price: $10.99

For these and other resources contact your local Christian Book Center

ABC
www.adventistbookcenter.com

or Berean Books
P. O. Box 2799,
Ann Arbor, MI 48197
Tel. 1-800-423-1319
www.berean-books.org

AUTHOR'S BOOK ON LOVE

Love. It's the never-ending, driving quest—theee all-consuming need—the motivating desire—of every man, woman, and child on earth.

But just what *is* love? Is it accurately defined by the sum total of all the song lyrics, love poems, and love stories ever written? All the movies ever filmed? All the dramas ever acted?

Toward a deeper, more satisfying answer to the question "What is love?" the *This Is Love* book manuscript contains a distilled, carefully chosen sampling of poems, quotations, articles and essays, stories, and personal reflections focused on love.

Some of the material in these pages is original to the author. Some represents the best thoughts of other writers. Found here are the words of those divinely inspired and those who have simply shared their own ideas.

But in a search for the true definition of love, where this *This Is Love* book best succeeds is in its undeviating focus on the Source of all real love—the One whose name is synonymous with love.

Real love cannot exist outside of a relationship. And whether ours is horizontal, involving other people around us—or vertical, between us and our God—or both, this book will open new vistas of understanding and delight as readers take in its pages

NOT FOR